EPIDEMIC LEADERSHIP

How to Lead *Infectiously* in the Era of Big Problems

EPIDEMIC LEADERSHIP

LARRY McEVOY, MD

WILEY

Published by John Wiley & Sons, Inc., Hoboken, New Jersey.
Published simultaneously in Canada.

Library of Congress Cataloging-in-Publication Data is Available:

ISBN 9781119787457 (Hardcover)
ISBN 9781119787471 (ePDF)
ISBN 9781119787464 (ePub)

Cover Design: Wiley
Cover Image: Courtesy of LCI Group, LLC

SKY10028214_071621

For the joyous crowds, the great herds, the endless flocks, the teeming schools (of fish and children), and all whose goodness incubates in obscurity ahead of coming abundance

Contents

Introduction

When I started writing this book, epidemics didn't hold the attention of many people beyond epidemiologists and risk-policy wonks. Then, COVID-19 hit. By a freak of timing, I found myself writing as the pandemic ended hundreds of thousands of lives, closed our schools and workplaces, crashed the global economy, monopolized the daily news cycle, and drove us out of the open and into hiding, from our parks and streets and deeper into our screens and phones. Like all of us, I watched as the spread of a brainless virus exploited our societal divisions and inequalities, exposed the inadequacy of leadership and supply lines, and tilted a presidential election. A microscopic clump of genetic material enveloped in proteins made the reality of epidemics a palpable threat and an urgent teacher. It challenged our notions of command and control over our environment and opened the possibilities around what leading must become in a changed and changing world.

I write from my perspective as a doctor and particularly as an emergency physician. My clinical career began as a medical student at Stanford University and took root in the garden of pathology we call the emergency department during my residency at Hennepin County Medical Center in Minneapolis. I learned the highly specialized skills that allowed me to diagnose, treat, and resuscitate patients whose unpredictable palette of disease, distress, and destruction flowed into my workplace every day, night, and weekend. Over the course of my clinical career, I learned to find a sense of ease amid the chaos of lives abruptly unhinged from the illusion of "normal." I learned that high-trust team intelligence outpaced disconnected expertise. I learned that all the algorithms and protocols in the world don't equip us to match the way disease and illness multiply in our populations, a reality our health care personnel recognized only too well from the strain on them during this most recent pandemic.

I also write from the perspective of an executive who has worked with hundreds of leaders and teams over the course of my career. I had the opportunity to help an emergency department and two health care organizations work their way through duress and subpar performance to results both objectively demonstrated and subjectively immeasurable. As the CEO of my state's largest trauma center, I watched several thousand people turn an entire organization around when it was listing badly during the national financial meltdown of 2008 (and when cynics predicted our inevitable collapse). Perhaps befitting an emergency physician and others who find themselves facing the braver work of leadership, I have always worked and learned in places where what used to work doesn't anymore, where people are trying hard and wearing out, and where hope is essential and hard to find.

We live in such times and places today. We have too much to do and not enough time to do it. Our technology ambiguously speeds things along and rushes us so fast we can't think straight. Our models of organization, leadership, and governance are breaking down, or at least groaning and cracking, under the weight of problems that are large, complex, and interconnected. Our world, whether we measure it in divisiveness, environmental degradation, or the vitality of our workplaces and communities, grows unhealthier and more stressed. The future arrives and beckons our response, yet we resist. Leaders have to grapple with all these things in a way that enables people to deliver better results, to learn relentlessly, and to re-energize and reconnect. Somehow those things have to happen not once, not in a few places, but repetitively, everywhere.

Along came coronavirus, specifically SARS-CoV-2, an obscure idea of a germ morphed into a worldwide infectious, political, social disruption with catastrophic and fracturing consequences. No more hiding. It's in our face, *here and real*. It has threatened our bodies, rattled our minds, split our towns and neighborhoods, and shocked our systems. More quietly, it has asked us if we're ready, really ready, to accept a present reality that invites a powerful shift to a better future.

Epidemics represent and expose the scientific principles underlying networks, complex systems, biology, and, in the case of humans, neurobiology. Such disciplines are rife with research, complex mathematical and statistical formulations, and underlying concepts of physics and biology that can be bewildering. This book is not meant to be an in-depth scientific exegesis. Instead, it is intended as an invitation to think about leading with a new framework, a framework that unfolds into simple, accessible concepts and techniques that leaders can put to work wherever they are to create both individual participation and collective wisdom in a world where scaling both stability and adaptability has become non-negotiable.

The unsettling reality is that epidemics are here to stay; they're going to keep coming, and not just because of wet markets in China and close-clustered human populations and degraded habitats where long-locked pathogens can get loose, leap to us, and multiply across the globe. We have invited and designed a world of networks and swarms, and now we will have to adapt. Our computing power lives in clouds and networks; our social momentum rides on platforms and movements of easily accessible information and even more accessible—and influential—disinformation. Our small local worlds are linked, and the uptake and spread of ideas and actions—healthy and unhealthy—defines leading and following today.

These realities of the modern world—call it "high-velocity, high-volatility," VUCA, Industry 4.0, or just the twenty-first century—raise compelling questions for leaders.

- How do we deal with phenomena that come from nowhere and end up everywhere?
- How do we respond and act with agility without rushing ourselves into regressive patterns? How do we match the speed of what is coming at us while slowing down enough to create wide patterns of insight and intention?

- What do we keep, discard, and learn anew from a leadership perspective? What works and what doesn't anymore? How do we know?
- What do we need to understand to shape a positive future in our lives, teams, companies, and world?

The powerful possibilities are perhaps most compelling. We think, sensibly enough, about stopping epidemics, limiting their damage, returning to normal. At first glance—and second and third—the coronavirus is simply badness, destruction, hindrance. It exposes our operational bottlenecks, our leadership division, our social inequities. Look deeper, and it carries a leadership blueprint for effective action in a connected world.

If I have learned one thing in my lifetime of work as a doctor and a leader, it is that the world is abundant with good ideas and good people. I am only a single searcher of the billions of people who seek better ideas and ways, and I find them every day and everywhere—in the ER in the middle of the night, in slums in Africa, in schools and basketball teams, in start-ups and bureaucracies. Too often those ideas and people stay hidden and "uninfectious." We need them to rise now, to go epidemic and flood into every nook and cranny where their humble origins can metastasize into florid impact.

I have learned a great deal from the patients I have cared for and from the people who taught me and mentored me (which would include those conventionally labeled "followers"). I learned a great deal also from decades of long days out in bad weather and good in my Montana homeland, where the ubiquitous surging of living things defined my experience and shaped my subsequent thoughts. The science of my profession and the land of my upbringing have helped me understand the beauty and wisdom in biology. Amid a world that has ignored the lessons of biology for too long, my hope now is to share a bit of what biology knows to participate in an epidemic of good.

This book is about our changing concept of leadership in a century when things move faster and overwhelm sooner, where anything can become very big very quickly, and each of us can feel very small. This book is about how leaders can shape and scale both stability and adaptation far beyond their individual contact points; as such, it is also a book about the design and ethic of social power. The epidemics we face, whether Ebola or COVID-19, whether QAnon or racism or opioids, are not going away. Indeed, conditions are set that will invite them to flourish and erupt.

This book has two sections. The first section builds from the universal experience of well-intentioned individuals who find themselves overwhelmed, starting with my sobering encounter with that reality as an emergency physician. Chapter 2 explores the potential advantages of how epidemics arise and grow for those who are encountering the "math problem" of personal effort in the face of diffuse and powerful obstacles. Chapter 3 delves into the implications of complex environments on what leadership does and how it will need to operate in our era of immense challenges. Chapter 4 explores the secret sauce of epidemics for leaders, the idea of self-organization that offers a flywheel to scaling the deliverables of leadership: performance, learning, and vitality.

The second section focuses on the practice of epidemic leadership and how leaders can design and sustain positive epidemics as systemic leverage in human systems. Chapter 5 emphasizes the identification of a positive pathogen as the basis of a constructive epidemic. Chapters 6 through 9 explore the elements of self-organization with respect to epidemics—conditions, interactions, and multipliers—with a special focus on networks and their unique capability to accelerate or obstruct leadership efforts. Chapter 10 explores the paradox of technology in supporting and complicating epidemic leadership. Finally, the type of thinking and the foundational sorts of social pathogens we need moving in today's world comprise Chapter 11, the final chapter.

The reason I write this book intertwines with the impact the pandemic meted out: the realities of our world are unsettling. I write this book because, as a doctor, anything that threatens the vitality of individuals, populations, and communities rouses my concern, and there are far more causes for concern than I could ever address as one lone healer. There is no single bedside I can rush to, no drug I can prescribe, no diagnostic algorithm I can wield. An ethic of healthy twenty-first-century community has to swarm everywhere—through our schools, our economies, our neighborhoods, our corporations, our conflicts, and our institutions. Many people would say such permeation is not possible. But somewhere, in or near Wuhan, China, in late 2019, arose a virus that was nameless, without money or power, with no business plan or Twitter following, with no passport and no cognition—and now it's everywhere, because we passed it among ourselves.

The good news about our current reality is that we have the knowledge and access to exploit these same conditions to create innumerable positive epidemics. It is not just time to lead in the middle of an epidemic, to prevent the next one, or to arrest bad ones. It is time to lead *like* an epidemic, launch multiple epidemics, and have an epidemic of leaders who know how to "epidemic."

Understanding Epidemics

1 My No Good, Very Bad Night in the Emergency Department

You're gonna need a bigger boat.
—Amity Island Police Chief Martin Brody in Jaws

Friday Night in the Emergency Department

August 15, 2003, Billings, Montana

We begin in illness and injury. On this hot Friday evening, patients swamp the emergency department in the regional trauma center where I work. In the late summer heat, the night is just starting and has already flooded us with a raft of patients, and it promises to keep building. The waiting room overflows with more people. I have worked hundreds of nights like these in the previous decade plus, and I know the pattern. The quiet heat and the coming sunset belie the more ominous certainty of my shift ahead. People would get sick, some dramatically so. People would die. No one had gone about their day thinking these things would happen, but we know. In the emergency department, we check our equipment and ready ourselves with certainty.

As I cross the threshold of the automatic double doors into the department to begin my shift, I know it's busy even without scanning the electronic register we call "the board," a remnant of the days when we used to list each patient and their chief complaints in bright dry erase marker on a big whiteboard before privacy concerns made it obsolete. I can hear the beeping of monitors, the shift in cadence of nurses' feet, and a low kind of ER buzz. The source is hard to pinpoint, like the low but incessant sound of unseen insect wings. To a casual observer, the department seems quiet, orderly, bright with fluorescent light. We like it that way—who wants to work in, let alone be sick in, a chaos of noise and motion?

The full cornucopia of unexpected disaster and discomfort bubbles out of the streets and homes and open spaces of life in America and flows into every room in our emergency department: automobile trauma, diabetes, cardiovascular disease, emphysema, diverticulitis, stroke, assault, cervical cancer, migraines, lacerations, domestic abuse, and opioids. The terms are medical and numbingly antiseptic, but the reality is stark: as the people of my town enjoy the warm summer evening, they are also crashing, dying, bleeding, fighting, and writhing in droves. While they go about their daily lives, they are part of a large, oddly silent tsunami of ill health that washes over the entire population.

No one is catastrophically ill at the moment, so I ease into my shift, getting labs and X-rays started on a few patients while I mentally accept that we will be working behind for a few hours. No one on the team likes working from behind. We prefer to stay ahead of the wave, seeing people as they come in. It is safer that way, and psychically easier for us. When the wave breaks over us, when we get behind, delays pile up and surprises happen, and surprises mean a higher chance of bad things for patients. Some nights, despite our best efforts, especially hot ones on summer weekends, the wave breaks, and we are playing catch-up. Tonight is one of those nights. The department has been behind since the afternoon, and it will be several more hours before we can get on top of the wave again.

The patients are varied, which is normal for us. The ER is the funnel for anything that can go wrong anywhere, at any time, for anybody. I see an obese patient whose knees hurt, a woman with vaginal bleeding, a middle-aged man with chest pain, a mom with back pain who can't lie down comfortably, an 80-year-old man with bad lungs. Nothing out of the ordinary, except I see all those people in the first 15 minutes, because twice that many wait unseen after that. I use my "30 seconds to meaningful rapport" to inspect and connect with each person I see. My trained eye scans breathing dynamics, skin color, tone of voice. I see eyes and facial expressions, plumb for fear or hidden motivations, search for the best way to settle every person who meets me for the first time in this place that is their bad detour and my daily work. My hands find theirs, and I rest them on shoulders and knees.

I step out of an older man's room into the low hum and look right, then left. I am impressed and grateful for what I see in the team of nurses, techs, registration clerks, and my emergency physician colleague seeing patients alongside me. Several years before, we weren't so much a seamless round-the-clock clinical team as a collection of technically proficient individuals. We couldn't elevate our game in the face of unrelenting pace. We didn't work that well together, and we weren't able to mesh the technical craft of our job with the human presence of connecting to each and every person who was ill, whatever their circumstances.

Eight years later, almost everything is different. More people come to us for care, and the metrics that define "good department" are positive: patient satisfaction and staff engagement have rebounded to high numbers from low ones, safety and quality metrics are strong, and the department sustains itself financially. Nurses are on a waiting list to get a position in the ED from other places in the hospital. Patients come by foot and ambulance, airplane and helicopter. Thank you notes dot the bulletin board in our break room, some with pictures of healed patients on vacations or hikes in the nearby Beartooth Mountains. Nurses, techs, and physicians work hard to help each other across the shift: quiet high-fives, thank-yous, and smiles pepper our interactions.

This night, we are at the top of our game. The patients are getting attentive and skilled care, and the team works fluidly without stress under the pressure of pace and pathology, moving fast without hurrying. We flex and bend to the needs of each patient and the staccato flow of the pace. As an emergency physician, I am at the peak of my craft. Well-trained and supported by capable nurses and skilled physicians alike, taught by thousands of patients, I am in the sweet-spot overlap of state-of-the-art training and sufficient experience, eight years out of a leading residency in my specialty of emergency medicine. I am comfortable on such weekend nights, at ease with the people I work with, the maladies and mishaps I would see, my own strengths and gaps as a clinician.

Despite the team's skill and my experience, a creeping dread wells within me as I scan up and down the hallway. It is my birthday, and while I am used to working holidays of all kinds and at all hours, this particular moment collides jarringly with all my years of effort, learning, triumphs, mistakes, hopes, and deaths in an unsettling pang in my gut and chest. In every room in our emergency department that night, while the ill and injured are getting what they need and we are chewing steadily at the backlog of patients piling into the waiting room, a bigger problem waits—no, *grows*—outside and beyond, unhurried, unstoppable, and inevitable. Nowhere does this unsettling gloom stick more than in my nose. The smell of blood, alcohol, feces, urine, antiseptic wipes, plastic tubing, vomit, and air freshener mix in my nasal cavity and settle like fine dust into my brain. Years before, when I was thinking of medicine and not yet doing it, I might have gagged. Now I just take a deep breath. It is not the smell of living.

"What you thinking, Scary Larry?" Dana, the charge nurse, appears at my elbow with a slight tug. "Big things or right-now things?"

She and I have worked together long enough to have earned our mutual nicknames for each other: Super Nurse and Scary Larry. I have worked with her while she handled two critically ill patients as the primary nurse while she held the charge nurse helm at the same time in the middle of the night. She can meet the wave. She knows my tendency to arc from micro-focus on the things at hand to macro meanderings on the source and end of what we see. She's more practical and fixes her mental gaze on getting through the shift.

"Big things," I say.

She smiles, and the tug turns into a nudge. "Keep moving. We can hear about it later when it quiets down." She gives me a wink before she moves past me: *Shifts don't run us, Scary Larry. You and me—we run them.*

As I suspected it would, the night swells into repeated waves of patients. They are unique and different individuals, but the patterns are familiar: strokes, heart attacks, overdoses, self-mutilation, asthma, domestic violence, rodeo mishaps, farm trauma, bar fights. I keep moving, patient to patient, through late Friday into early Saturday morning. Until then, I don't eat, and I don't go to the bathroom. Neither does anyone else on the team.

The shift eventually ebbs like all waves do, falling back quietly into the night. By 4:30 in the morning, only two patients are left in the department. Both are resting, with no surprises lurking. One of them snores under a morphine blanket covering the pain of a broken leg, and the slow sound keeps the tempo of the deep night.

Five nurses and I sit at a round table a few feet behind the high counter of the nurses' station. I'm sifting through some blood and urine culture results from the lab, and they are getting ready to "count narcs," the frequent process of ensuring that all the potentially addictive drugs we use are all accounted for. I am reminded of being in a duck blind as a young boy with my dad, waiting out of the wind for ducks to sail in and disturb the quiet water around us.

"Good work, everyone. We cleaned up that board nicely," Dana says. She pulls out her auburn ponytail and redoes it. "And now, Scary Larry, what were those big thoughts bouncing around in your head while we were all moving so fast last night?"

"I was just thinking we're getting killed. What's outside that door is growing faster than we can keep up." I saw them looking at me. One of them rolled her eyes. "And it's getting bigger, not better."

"What are you talking about?" Mavis had been in the department a long time. She grew up on a wheat farm in eastern Montana and had worked hard her whole life. "Five years ago it would have taken us a whole day to get through what we just did in eight hours. We were rolling."

I smiled even as my bones felt heavy with fatigue. "It's not that. We run a shift just fine. Better and better every day, really. But society creates more disease, manufactures it actually, faster than we can keep up. The harder and better we work, the farther behind we are against a disease burden that's getting bigger, not smaller. Not in the shift, not in the department, but in the big picture. You ever have that feeling?"

"All the time . . . and then I stop thinking about it," said Kim. "It's too much for me. Too big. I just think about my kids and my family and try to be a good nurse."

"What did you expect? It's an emergency department," Judy said. "People get sick and injured in more ways than anyone could imagine, and we pick up the pieces." Judy had worked in the department for 15 years. In her view, humans were fallen and flawed creatures, and we suffered the consequences.

"I think of it as job security," said Shelly. A couple years later, she would be a nurse practitioner and would leave us for the cardiology department. "No illness, no disaster, no job."

The Problem That Won't Go Away

They were right and sane and rational, of course, those exquisitely capable nurses in the middle of the night at the tail end of a busy shift. Living and working at the back end of a massive bloom of unhealth and disease tends to make us feel very small. Think about it too much, and you go nuts. You can only go without food and bathroom breaks for so long. You have a job and a family and a life. The shift ends and you have to get some sleep.

Yet the question remains: What will we do about these "too big things"?

As good as we were that shift in August 2003, we were falling behind then, and we are falling behind now. The prevalence of illness we were dealing with that night was—and still is—ominous and exponential: we have epidemics of obesity, high blood pressure, domestic violence, opioids, anxiety, cervical cancer, smoking, meth, HIV, teenage suicide, disinformation.

We have created fancy, distancing words for these things—disease burden, pathology, psychosocial determinants of health—but up close, staring at you with sweaty foreheads and bluish lips, gushing out of wounds, groaning from half-opened mouths, these words cannot sterilize the sensory experience: sickness is on the move.

We spend hundreds of millions of dollars creating a vaccine for influenza every year, educating people, holding flu shot clinics, and influenza still erupts *every single year*. Worse, when you look at what causes illness and death, lost wages and jobs, lost productivity and the high societal cost of health care, you find a sobering truth: we are creating the epidemics we are trying to stop. They are not mere accidents.

As a doctor intent on creating the reversal of injury, the return to health, some sort of positive impact for and with the patients I cared for, the scale of it drowned me that night in 2003. I had been trained to treat disease and injury, to pull alongside ailing people and, with my hard-earned priestly wisdom and science and human compassion, help them restore themselves. Sometimes it worked, sometimes it didn't, but I had not anticipated that the exponential surge of these things would overwhelm not just me, but all of us. I had been taught that the combination of technical knowledge, well-designed and well-practiced process, and collaborative teamwork was the answer. If not, then sleep deprivation, skipping meals, and not going to the bathroom until the shift was over would surely do the trick.

Was I being foolish to believe the unspoken promise of my training and mentors? Had I been sold a naïve myth unsuited for a cynical world?

That birthday night when the overwhelming reality of what was flowing through the ER doors crystallized in my awareness, I was neither a novice doctor nor an entry-level leader. I had chaired our department as we rose on the efforts and ideas of a hundred people from an apathetic culture and subpar quality to a place patients flocked to when they got sick. I was a senior executive in our larger organization as it was on its way to becoming *Consumer Reports*' number-one safety organization in 2012.

I had been "leadership developed" since high school and would be throughout my entire executive career. I had been tested, tooled, evaluated, lectured, boot camped, accredited, certified, promoted, fed-back, coached, videotaped, and fish-bowled. In response to the question, "What do you want to focus on?" at a leadership institute, I replied that I wanted to understand how to go from linear to logarithmic, to understand how to move entire systems so they could respond without relying on running people ragged as a workaround. I saw eyes widen—just barely, but I saw it—and then heard a hastily formed reply uttered in a soothing voice: "We start with ourselves, the only thing we really can control, and you can only do what you can do." Perfectly sensible.

Yet the flu rolls on, and so does Ebola, Zika, H1N1, MERS, SARS, and now COVID-19. And so does the exhaustion and the pace. In my native sector of health care, over 50 percent of physicians are burned out,[1] and the literature clearly shows how that physician epidemic impacts quality and cost, not to mention patients' lives, limbs, families, and peace of mind.[2] Over half of executives in health care would quit if they could.[3] If you lost 40 percent of your blood volume in short order, you would be experiencing what we call class IV hemorrhagic shock. We would consider that class of shock a collapse of the 300-trillion cell system known as you, defined by death unless a trauma team resuscitated you. We can see lots of "collapse" numbers like these—honeybees, cancer, environmental data, employee disengagement. The people I talk with—executives, small business owners, consultants, associates, partners, young, old—all note the same trend: things are moving so fast, there's not enough time in the day, and one little person cannot move these big rafts of inertia. Even if we could, we're all exhausted. According to a recent Gallup study, two out of three employees experience burnout at some point in their jobs, with secondary effects on their health and ability to function at home.[4]

Sleep-Deprived Insight

After the conversation with the nurses, patients began to trickle in as morning arrived. I finished the shift and drove home to where I lived west of town. I opened the ranch gate to our place and paused to take in the land where I lived. It was a quiet ritual of mine that created space between the sights and sounds of my job and the world of my family. Depending on which shift I had just worked, I took a few minutes under the stars or the bright sun to let the insights of the work settle in and to let the sometimes assaulting nature of it wash out onto the ground.

The bright morning air, still cool, held the hint of another hot day, and the slanting sun cast dark shadows on the sun-washed ponderosa coulees and grassy ridges. There is nothing better to wash the olfactory memory of alcohol, blood, urine, and pus from one's brain than the morning smell of sage and Ponderosa pine, nothing better to replace the beeping of monitors and moans of the sick than the breeze wandering in the grassy air. Surrounded by healthier sounds and sights in my sleep-deprived, almost-to-sleep ease, it struck me that the epidemics that cause such ill consequence among us—obesity, cardiovascular disease, HIV, gun violence—were playing by a different set of rules than the ones underlying how I had been taught to respond to them.

I stopped at the corral to feed our two horses. Randomly, my dad's offhand observation about why horses are beautiful wafted across my mind: *They've retained their wild shape.* We had bought our place six years before, and like so many of the patients I encountered in the emergency department, it was in a degraded state when we found it: overgrazed, eroded, barren of its original biodiversity, its history largely erased. Our hope was to help it heal, and if the ER was an exercise in meeting people in an arc of health that I might never see again, the land was an arc that stayed with me and under my feet, beginning long before me and extending far after. Although the grass crunched yellow in the high summer of a 10-year drought, the ecosystem was surging back to health, not falling behind. Life was recovering here: grasses and shrubs were rebounding, insects and birds were returning, water and soil were recharging. If the ER shift had exhausted me with its physical pace and psychic implications, the sights and smells of the land in the sunny morning inspired and soothed.

I had grown up here in this place of big land and teeming life, raised and surrounded by people who had me in it early and often. I had long wondered how the elegance of biology, so essential to the enduring vitality of every person and every living thing on this planet, did not seem to translate to how we designed organizations, leadership approaches, team dynamics, or even our internal mindsets. The exponential trends that bedeviled me as a doctor and inspired me as a landowner were playing by biological rules; our responses seemed to be so much more mechanical and rigid. And slower. And ineffective. And falling behind.

In the fuzzy haze of near-sleep consciousness I would endure for another 30 minutes before I crashed onto my pillow, a meandering thought surfaced for the first time: if epidemics organize and spread by different, biological rules, what if we could harness the rules and link them to positive realities—to cures, to answers, to ideas, to swarms of positive impact? If I was serious about health, if I was serious about understanding how to multiply adaptive capacity in the face of too much to do and not enough time to do it, I was going to have to answer—positively—the question posed by the epidemics that flowed across the threshold of the ED in that unstoppable wave. How could we create positive phenomena that spread just as powerfully, exponentially, into every nook and cranny, the way epidemics overwhelm our defenses against them?

I wasn't thinking of epidemics as leadership that morning. I only knew at that time that I was on the right side of wanting to be helpful and the wrong side of the way things launched, grew, spread, and moved. From the patients I attended to the land I lived on, I understood biology held vitalizing, relentless capacity. Beyond that, I was out of ideas, and I was too long without sleep.

I went down into the darkest room in my house and fell into the motionless, dreamless sleep of the night worker.

Notes

1. Tait D. Shanafelt, MD, et al., "Changes in Burnout and Satisfaction with Work-Life Balance in Physicians and the General US Working Population Between 2011 and 2014," *Mayo Clinic Proceedings* 90, no. 12 (December 1, 2015): 1600–1613, https://doi.org/10.1016/j.mayocp.2015.08.023.
2. Maria Panagioti et al., "Association Between Physician Burnout and Patient Safety, Professionalism, and Patient Satisfaction: A Systematic Review and Meta-analysis," *JAMA Internal Medicine* 178, no. 10 (October 1, 2018): 1317–1331, https://doi.org/10.1001/jamainternmed.2018.3713.
3. "The Impact of Burnout on Healthcare Executives: A WittKieffer Study," WittKieffer.com, online survey conducted summer 2018, https://www.wittkieffer.com/thought-leadership/impact-of-burnout-on-healthcare-executives-witt-kieffer-study/.
4. Ben Wigert and Sangeeta Agrawal, "Employee Burnout, Part 1: The 5 Main Causes," *Gallup Workplace,* July 12, 2018, https://www.gallup.com/workplace/237059/employee-burnout-part-main-causes.aspx.

2 The Good Epidemic—Really?

Nature does not hurry, yet everything is accomplished.

—Lao Tzu

Good People, Bad Disease

In 2008, several years removed from my discouraging night in the ER, I took a role as the CEO of what was then Colorado's largest trauma center. I entered an organization rife with internal strife and external pressures. I had to familiarize myself quickly with a new organization, five thousand new colleagues, teammates, and opinions, and a city-owned health system in a national financial meltdown. Three days' worth of cash on hand stood between us and our debt holders' right to come in and run the place, and we had $320 million of bond debt tied up in the auction-rate bond market, which collapsed midyear, leaving us with worthless and burdensome debt and no bank willing to help us restructure it. Our compliance with federal guidelines was suspect at best, and the penalties for compliance violations were high and included incarceration of the "designated jailable officer"—me. Our finances were sagging after five years of investing in a new hospital with gorgeous brick and glass without replacing the numerous pieces of expensive technology that were reaching the end of their life cycles.

Nationally, we were entering a recession, which always decreases traffic to hospitals and clinics, and our city, strapped for cash as a sales-tax municipality, was hoping we would fund the city's budget, either by funneling cash flow or by selling the organization. All over the country, cities, states, and the nation itself puzzled constantly over how to fund health care, and I had landed in a town that wanted health care to fund the city.

We had no firm plan for working with physicians to improve and innovate the clinical care. Relationships with and between physicians themselves were poor, rife with manipulative competition, collegial distrust, and a long history of triangulation with the hospital's need to keep beds full. Within a month of my arrival, a patient told a nurse he was having a heart attack, and, despite repeated attempts by him and his family to tell us how ill he was, we only figured it out a few hours later when he died. The physicians blamed the nurses, the nurses blamed each other, and everyone blamed administration.

We had too much to fix and not enough time to do it. We had lots of policies and no consistent practices. We had lots of opinions and very little shared insight. People were hoarding clinical supplies in closets and above the ceiling tiles. We lacked operating processes, procedural rigor, and cultural alignment. We had chaos.

On top of safety risks, lagging results, and broken processes in the setting of a crashing economy, we had a more ominous problem. As I walked the halls and spoke with doctors, nurses, clerks, and pharmacists, I kept hearing we had a leadership problem. From leaders, I kept hearing we had "the wrong people." I also kept hearing from people who had worked there a long time, who loved the place, and who wanted to be very good at their jobs. They took great pride in their professions and truly wanted to help people. When I asked them what they thought we needed to do to address the woes we were experiencing, I received a lot of head shakes, eye rolls, and muttering, but they all sent the same message: "This place can't change. Don't even try. It's been this way for years. You'll see."

We had an internal lean coach named Jauna Werner who had arrived a bit before I did. She was skilled in facilitating shifts to lean thinking, but she was even more astute as an observer of all the little things that underpinned how a system was functioning. As she rounded through the organization, looking at operational processes and listening to people, she had come to an interesting conclusion.

"This place could benefit a lot from lean, but not yet. It needs therapy first. Maybe gene therapy." We had all the hallmarks of a degraded ecosystem. Performance was sagging and widespread. Our ability to adapt was mired in entrenched frustration and apathy. Our biodiversity of thought and perspective had been winnowed to a few surviving patterns, and energy was low.

I spoke to and listened to hundreds of people. From a clinical perspective, I was fascinated with the ubiquitous combination of personal commitment and collective malaise. From an executive perspective, I sensed that we could fix all the policies, processes, and protocols we wanted, but until we got at the more foundational, lurking source of will in the organization, we would be wishing for results rather than creating them. I had a big whiteboard in my office, and after a month or so of scrawling on it with notes, pictures, and network diagrams in different colored markers, I wrote in big red letters with a circle around them, "CPD."

The Epidemic Inevitable

Until COVID-19 shattered our veneer, many of us thought of epidemics as relics of the past, or at least something not particularly relevant to our day-to-day lives. We have an annual influenza epidemic, and in the twenty-first century we've already had epidemics of diseases with strange names: SARS, MERS, Zika. Ebola, the virus lurking in the equatorial forests of Africa, rose up and killed 11,310 people in Guinea, Liberia, and Sierra Leone between 2014 and 2016.[1] That was then, though, we thought. It was so long ago and far away in an age when yesterday can be quickly forgotten. Our world kept whirring in a blur of Facebook posts, hypershort media cycles, and a million things to do and distract before COVID arrived. Possessed of our computers and networks, vaccines and antibiotics, constant video feeds and big data, it was tempting to see the deadly power of epidemics as old furniture in remotely historic eras—if we were even thinking about epidemics at all.

There were, indeed, catastrophic and legendary eruptions of disease in the past. Across history, infectious plagues have certainly decimated humanity—the biblical plagues, the Black Death, the flu epidemic of 1918. Smallpox, now officially eradicated, killed as many as 300 million people in the twentieth century alone,[2] despite the fact that vaccination against it began in the early 1800s. Unknown millions of people native to the Western Hemisphere died after Columbus brought the disease to the New World in 1492.[3] Those sweeping sixteenth-century North American epidemics, while hinted at by later smallpox outbreaks, remain largely invisible to our subsequent awareness as they weren't recorded. Instead, vastly reduced populations of Indigenous people defined the modern view of the Western Hemisphere's human numbers as more Europeans arrived later to a vastly underpopulated continent.[4]

Bubonic plague, the infamous Black Death, entered Europe in 1347 after the disease inserted itself into a year-long siege between the Mongol King Jariberg and Italian merchants at the outpost of Cappra. Once it reached mainland Europe, 25–50 million people died in five years, thought to be 50 percent of Europe's population at the time. Then, as now, adjacent unrest and violence flared up, as antisemitic sentiment and brutality boiled to the surface. Over 200 Jewish communities were massacred; 2000 Jewish people were burned alive in Strasbourg alone on Valentine's Day, 1349.[5]

COVID may have surprised us, but it shouldn't have. We had warning that epidemics were looming. For some years, epidemiologists, scientists, and military planners have been warning us of the destabilizing power of epidemics moving through our populations. *Time Magazine's* 2017 cover declared, "*We Are Not Ready for the Next Pandemic*," and Bill Gates's now-famous TED Talk reviewed our urgent need to prepare for an era when tiny, anonymous microbes would sweep across our social stability and wreak upheaval. Before COVID arrived among us, Ebola, SARS, MERS, Zika, and H1N1 had already created significant havoc in the first fifth of the twenty-first century.

Epidemiologists tell us there are more epidemics ahead. Even now, while we grapple with logistic, economic, and political dimensions of the most widespread global health threat we have seen, policy makers, militaries, governments, health agencies, and intelligence capacities around the world are thinking about how to mitigate the devastation of "Disease X," the hypothetical viral pathogen poised to destabilize civilization. They contemplate the odds and possibilities of the kind of things that spawn horror movies—*World War Z, Outbreak, Contagion* all being examples of out-of-control instability that deadly epidemics bring. Can you imagine a virus that moves like COVID-19 and has Ebola's death rate of 50 percent? Those future superpathogens and their destructive fallout are what haunt the epidemiologists and military planners.

Approximately 1.67 million viruses are known to human science, for example. Over 250 of those infect humans, but scientists calculate there are between 631,000 and 827,000 viruses that can *potentially* infect humans.[6] In conditions of disruption and chaos—rapid environmental changes, degraded sanitation and nutrition, infrastructural decay, and social instability—such viruses are more likely to break out of their native environments, where they are locked into a kind of lattice that prevents them from causing human harm, into human populations. When these viruses do break out, they're lethal and expensive. Our pre-COVID twenty-first-century epidemics of SARS, Ebola, and Zika have all cost thousands of lives and tens of billions of dollars. The economic cost of COVID, of course, has been staggering. In a *Journal of the American Medical Association* article published in October of

2020 and based on the assumption that COVID-19 would be under control by the Fall of 2021, the authors estimated the cost of the epidemic at 16 *trillion* dollars.[7] That article was published before a number of the subsequent unknowns inherent in epidemics popped up—the vaccines, the mutations, the distribution delays. However accurate or inaccurate the estimate, the underlying point is clear: *disease-ridden societies cannot prosper.*

Viruses are particularly fantastic epidemic starter material, and Disease X refers specifically to viral pathogens, but epidemics don't have to be viral. Bacteria like streptococcus, the ubiquitous bug that infects human throats and causes the familiar childhood strep infection, and microscopic animals called protozoans, responsible for malaria, for example, can all move rapidly through human populations with devastating effect.

Those are just biological epidemics. We also now know epidemics can be behavioral and social, following the same organizing rules as purely biological ones. Authors such as Nicholas Christakis and James Fowler, who wrote a wonderful book called *Connected: The Surprising Power of Our Social Networks,* and Damon Centola, who wrote *How Behavior Spreads: The Science of Complex Contagions*, have revealed how behavioral epidemics both follow the rules of biological epidemics and also run counter to them in some ways. Although there are similarities and differences, the epidemics themselves are quite real.

These "believe-and-behave" epidemics are moving through our population with sinister effects. Opioid addiction is a classic example, but racism, antivaccine thinking, disinformation, QAnon, and online hate speech all follow the rules of epidemic spread within our human populations, apparently undaunted by our conventional efforts to stop them. Our social communities inherently unleash or corral ideas, insights, bias, and behaviors—voting tendencies, sexual practices, culinary recipes—much the way ecosystems unleash, stabilize, or inhibit infectious diseases.

Our communication technology has emerged as the double-edged sword to traffic both the profound evolution of ideas and the tragic deconstruction of social discourse. We once thought of epidemics as punishment from the Divine and then learned to triumph over them with vaccines and drugs. We now live in a world where the design of social media platforms both complicates our response to societal challenges and spawns whole clouds of thought and opinion, amplifying particular bits of information and—more ominously—disinformation. We have a measles vaccine, for example, that works well and can stop the disease of measles, a disease both highly contagious and significantly damaging. Unfortunately, we have a parallel epidemic of anti-vaccine thinking that undermines valid science and exploits vulnerable populations as effectively as any virus, leaving them swept with measles at a time when we have an effective vaccine to prevent it. Online, you can find both cogent scientific comment about the various COVID vaccines and maddeningly false but heavily trafficked myths about them. We've built a world where epidemics are inevitable and primed to be more explosive and more divisive.

We also know that where there is one epidemic, it's often riding on the coattails of another, or, if not, it spins off another one because of its own effects. Scientists call such pairings and linkages *syndemics.* Chlamydia and gonorrhea ride together, coexisting because of their similar method of sexual transmission. Similarly, COVID and obesity synergize in the United States, mixing to create a multiplying effect of severe illness, side effects, and death more pronounced than either would alone in the short term.[8]

Epidemics of skeptical mindsets and harmful behaviors have commingled amid COVID—those who thought the disease was a hoax were much more likely to flout practices that would limit its impact and spread, thereby unwittingly multiplying the phenomenon they didn't think was real. Because we do not pay so much attention to them when they're small and fragile, epidemics seem to just pop up, ooze under our doors, and grow. Once they get bigger and more widespread, they are much harder to reel back. Worse, epidemics spawn secondary epidemics. They literally multiply their own numbers and the numbers of problems they create.

We all want these epidemics to stop, to go away and never come back. But they don't. We have managed to eliminate a few, smallpox being the poster child for disease eradication, but most are stubborn and relentlessly reappearing. Influenza is a classic example, returning every year when the time is right. Equipped with maddeningly adaptive changes in its DNA sequencing that allow it to slip past both our engineered barriers—the annual version of the flu vaccine and our advocacy programs for getting a flu shot—and our bodily surveillance—our individual immune systems—it is relentless among us. There are other epidemics on which we have made great progress only to be foiled by an additive perceptual epidemic that has mitigated our efforts to stop the disease itself, as is the case with measles and antivaccine sentiment.

We've seen all these intertwined realities with COVID, and the take-home message for leaders is less about COVID itself, bad as it is, and more about the pattern of epidemic action in our social identity, large and small. We now know more about how epidemics rise, propagate, and abate, but the patterns are as timeless as biology, and they are not going away. The epidemics I was battling were not new to me or to science on my overwhelming night in the emergency department. We had been seeing gonorrhea, chlamydia, and influenza for years; we had also been seeing obesity, diabetes, domestic violence, and opioid use advancing across our populations.

It turns out epidemics are not just past and present; they are also future. Epidemics are not rare; they're common. Epidemics are not hypothetical; they're real. Born of disruption, they launch from a thousand places and cause more disruption. Epidemics aren't just throwing us into chaos but depend on and benefit from that chaos to rise and move. With our dense and redundant networks of travel, trade, and communication, we've built a world in which they will rise and rise again. They can and will be devastating.

Negative to Positive

After all the unwinding of what we considered stable and normal by COVID-19, the idea of emulating an epidemic, rather than fighting one, sounds almost sociopathic. Beyond understanding the dynamics of misery, is there anything to learn from these sprawling, creeping, relentless phenomena? Can understanding epidemics shed light on how we might lead positively, effectively, and exponentially in a world where disruption, velocity, and uncertainty bloom in the fields of "new normal" or the "new abnormal"? Can epidemics teach us, not just warn us? Can we learn to lead like them, not just in the face of them?

Yes.

Epidemics are not just negative and devastating; they can be positive and empowering. They surf on the same principles of social networks and multiply via the same organizing elements that leaders can use to positive advantage. What differentiates the value of an epidemic is its pathogen, its "disease maker," the thing that is multiplied and spread across a population. While the duration of a pathogen's effects and how fast or slow it spreads are adjuncts of whether we see an epidemic as "bad" or "good," the kernel of its value lies in its *founding idea*, which can unfold in unforeseeable combinations across populations. Bad ideas cause bad epidemics as they spread through our linked social networks, themselves powered by neural and technological networks; good ideas can seed good epidemics via the same approaches.

Ebola kills 50 percent, more or less, of the people who have it, and it's highly contagious, easily leaping from person to person unless you take active and repetitive precaution. Although we might consider a hypothetical disease called "Ebola lightweight" "better" if it were very difficult to pass from one person to the next and killed only 2 percent of those afflicted, the fundamental reality is that the Ebola virus is a recipe packet for human harm. On the other hand, innovation, collaboration, creativity, and empathy are action-ideas we would love to see bloom into epidemics in multiple places where they are currently missing. Although biological and behavioral epidemics are both different and similar, what differentiates bad and good is not how the epidemic organizes and moves, but *what it carries*. Positive epidemics carry good "pathogens," or payloads, whereas bad epidemics carry bad ones.

As we might expect in a world filled with its share of ambiguity and trade-offs, some epidemics carry both. Malaria, for example, has the nasty effects of causing illness, organ damage, and death, but has also driven the genetic origin of a hemoglobin variant that provides resistance to malaria. That variant, in turn, carries the burden of sickle cell disease. Viruses themselves carry genes that have integrated into our own genome over generations. Some of these genes contain the coding for essentially human processes—gestation, for example.[9] As we shall see, designing or selecting the right payload is critical, as is the ability to design and facilitate uptake and diffusion—spread!—constructively matched to that payload or idea.

Instead of waiting for small ideas and particles to mushroom serendipitously into big problems, would it be possible to think of large-scale positive effect and then grow it from a tiny—and accessible—idea or action into a macro effect? What if leaders could conjure positive "idea pathogens" and then support their interactive trafficking into stable and impactful patterns by tapping how epidemics originate and move?

For a moment, let's imagine the promising power of positive epidemics. Get the words "bad," "devastating," "death," "disease," and "harmful" out of your head. Let's look not at the *effects* epidemics wreak upon our minds and bodies and social institutions, but at the way they work, their intrinsic properties.

Epidemics Spread Exponentially

Epidemics explode from almost nothing to spectacularly something because they grow via nonlinear dynamics. Epidemics are an effective way for apparently powerless things to create big effects. They have the capacity to start behind, catch up, and go way past expectations. Despite being made of tiny particles with a massive energy deficit relative to their target organisms, with immune systems and barriers arrayed against them, epidemics have mastered the transition from current state to future state, from the way things are to the way things will be when they are on the move. They are able to move their version of an idea, a pathogenic particle, quickly, from behind and insignificant to swarming and impactful. A friend of mine likes to say we're "late, late, late" on addressing our biggest problems. Epidemics, in their ability to move quickly from nothing to something, offer a way to catch up when we're *late, late, late*.

Because they are exponential, epidemics create enormous leverage. Influenza is a tiny particle of quasi-life, yet it can shift the steady state of each of our entire bodies, which themselves are collective systems of one hundred trillion cells. That's a serious return on investment! Every leader and team benefits from leverage. There are more metrics and goals, opportunities and challenges, and energy and time requirements than we can ever handle ourselves. That's why humans have organized themselves into communities where we can better survive, create, respond, prosper, and *live*. Families, churches, companies, and governments all embody some type of social leverage. The "novel coronavirus" causing COVID-19 possesses leverage in spades. We were not able to stop it from going exponential.

Epidemics Tap Local Resources

Epidemics survive and flourish by co-opting the abundant resources of the natural system in which they live. While they may sprawl across wide territory, they are never burdened by long and complicated supply lines. Epidemics possess very little start-up capital; they "own" very little internal resource. Influenza doesn't get into your body with its own energy—it enters passively and then cranks up your vast energy-making capacity to fuel its own multiplication and impact. There are caveats and trade-offs to how epidemics co-opt our resources: the more invisible and mild the pathogen, the faster and wider it moves. Epidemics that don't ensure sufficient health of hosts—at least for a time—to allow for further contagion are scary and have a higher death rate, but they're not very successful. Epidemics that kill hosts too quickly and in high percentages compromise their own path to massive coverage of a population.

Epidemics Are Adaptive: They Flourish Against Resistance and Surprise

No one wants epidemics to pop up, let alone spread, and yet . . . they do! Epidemics face layers of obstacle and resistance—formal structures, money, organized social programs, and finally, our own immune systems, which are designed to recognize them, hunt them down, kill them, and keep a record for the next time. Epidemics are not confined to a single plan; they're constantly changing their playbook. If they don't, they are no longer an epidemic—they're a *past* epidemic, and likely a small one. Leaders constantly encounter resistance. Epidemics must thrive on the situation at hand. If that situation changes, they rapidly shift, or they cease to exist.

Epidemics *have* to be agile and opportunistic. With so many things out to stop them, they adapt relentlessly and frequently or die quickly. Our lives as leaders may not appear to be quite so harsh, but our world demands adaptation and agility as a continuous capacity.

Epidemics Organize Themselves

Epidemics launch without analytics, business plans, or protocols, from simple principles to complex patterns and into networks of relationships. How many of us have been taught to trust the power of *self-organization*? After all, it doesn't seem to work in teenage closets or postholiday kitchens. Imagine if your team, your company, or your school *self-organized*? Oddly and truly, self-organization is a predominant form of getting things done in the universe and overwhelmingly so in the biological world. Leaders can harness self-organization effectively and easily if we are willing to understand its requirements.

Epidemics self-organize in complex settings by riffing endlessly on simple building blocks and clumping combinations into patterns. It is this clumping of simplicity that paradoxically underpins an epidemic's enviable adaptability and ability to thrive in a world of complexity. They just keep finding different combinations until they hit a winning formula, and they keep working it until something forces a change. In a complex world, simplicity turns out to be not just a brain saver but an essential design parameter for scaling both uniformity and infinite variety.

Epidemics Have "Distributed Intelligence"

Epidemics have no "boss" or "alpha particle"; they don't have a single "knockout point." Their power is spread across a diffuse population of tiny things. You can't stop an epidemic by stopping one viral particle or one bacterium, or even one case of a disease (unless it's the first case, but we are rarely that lucky). Leaders would love to have an approach that "couldn't be knocked out." Increasingly, we now have the science to design distributed intelligence in both our computing platforms and our human teams and organizations.

Epidemics Flower in Instability and Disruption

Epidemics originate and thrive in perturbations and messes, making them ideal prototypes for how we might use instability to advantage in this modern age. If the point of disruption is just that—more disruption—then ethical leaders have little to learn from this originating condition of epidemics. On the other hand, if instability is not going away in our world, if "back to normal" is less likely than "forward to healthy," leaders of all styles can amplify their own positive effects because of, not in spite of, instability. Epidemics flower when "normal" shatters; so can you and your work.

Epidemics Offer a Vaccine Against Narcissism (Unless They're Traffickers of It)

In a recent article out of the Stanford Graduate School of Business, the authors note the common placement of narcissists in essential and influential leadership positions with disastrous effects.[10] Those effects marry the pathology of narcissistic people with the flaw of single-point-source leadership models and mal-designed selection biases (which themselves can be epidemic). As multi-point source phenomena with multiple sources of power and influence, social epidemics protect organizations by integrating a kind of "participatory source code" as a hedge against the over influence of a particular personality type. In a positive epidemic, a solitary narcissistic leader cannot create the negative effects of point-source narcissism. Collective intelligence blunts the risk and effect of singular "anti-intelligence." Authoritarianism can certainly be its own epidemic, or rather the source of an epidemic of acquiescence; but a properly designed epidemic can blunt the rise of personality-based leaders.

The behavior of epidemics themselves rests in firm and accessible scientific principles that any leader can put to work, right now, in any environment, whatever your formal positional power. Epidemics appear with infinite variation and allow us to understand how to lead with analogous flexibility. Conversely, they all follow a similar structure and map and invite us to understand how to lead with simplicity and stability. What good things those would be embodied in leadership itself as an epidemic: *flexibility, stability, simplicity*.

These are serious times, potentially dark times. They are also fantastically open and potential times. We don't have to watch helplessly while the terrifying epidemics of our day wash over our collective well-being and institutional function. Sometimes epidemics cannot be stopped; sometimes they can. Sometimes the best answer is to overwhelm them with the same idea-trafficking, effect-multiplying, resistance-responding approach that epidemics already embody. Sometimes we don't need to wait for an epidemic to wake us up; we can spin them up, good ones, right where we are.

Leading this way is grounded in serious science, but that doesn't mean it has to be complicated or exhausting. It does mean taking a look at our assumptions about leading, organizing, and how things really get done sustainably and at scale. Your team, your company, your congregation, your community, and our world all wait.

Ready?

Seeking the Good Disease

In May 2008, a few months into my CEO tenure, Cari Davis, our marketing and communications director, stopped in one day and inspected my whiteboard scribbling. Cari had been born in the hospital and grew up in our community. She was educated on the East Coast, had served on the board, and had taken a position in the organization a couple years earlier. She and I had been talking about how our communication, both formal and informal, could reinforce old or new patterns in the organization's function.

"What is this?" she asked.

"It's a map. Of our disease." I pointed to various interconnected people, locations, and issues, outlined as dots and boxes with connecting lines. "I thought it was just here"—I pointed with my marker—"but then it showed up here"—I pointed again—"and then here. It's not every single person, but it's an awfully high percentage. It seems to be everywhere."

"What's the disease? '*We've always done it this way*'?"

"Oooh, I like that," I said. "But no. It's this." I pointed to the CPD lettered within the big circle. "I call it *Chronic Proliferative Dysphoria*."

"Sounds medical."

"It does," I said. "It's a silly little term I made up for our organizational syndrome: unhappy people creating more unhappiness and proliferating it across their work, constantly, to the detriment of our results, our ability to change, and our vitality. That's my doctor's diagnosis."

"You're right." She studied the circles and initials. "It *is* everywhere. So how do you cure something that's everywhere?"

"Not sure yet. Not by surgery. I am positive the high power of the CEO megaphone is *not* going to cure this disease. I wish we had a vaccine, but it's too late. We need to replace the bad disease with a good one. We have to find out what that good disease is. Yesterday."

Notes

1. "2014–2016 Ebola Outbreak in West Africa," Centers for Disease Control and Prevention, last reviewed March 8, 2019, `https://www.cdc.gov/vhf/ebola/history/2014-2016-outbreak/index.html`.
2. Colette Flight, "Smallpox: Eradicating the Scourge," BBC, last updated February 17, 2011, `https://www.bbc.co.uk/history/british/empire_seapower/smallpox_01.shtml`.
3. Donald A. Henderson, "The Eradication of Smallpox—an Overview of the Past, Present, and Future," *Vaccine* 29, suppl. 4 (December 30, 2011): D7–D9, `https://doi.org/10.1016/j.vaccine.2011.06.080`.
4. Charles C. Mann, *1491: New Revelations of the Americas Before Columbus* (New York: Alfred A. Knopf, 2005), 30; see figure.
5. John Seven, "The Black Death: A Timeline of the Gruesome Pandemic," History.com, accessed January 28, 2021, `https://www.history.com/news/black-death-timeline`.
6. Robert Kessler, "What Is Disease X?" *EcoHealth Alliance*, August 3, 2019, `https://www.ecohealthalliance.org/2018/03/disease-x`.
7. David M. Cutler, PhD, "The COVID-19 Pandemic and the $16 Trillion Virus," *JAMA* 324, no. 15 (October 20, 2020): 1495–1496, `https://jamanetwork.com/journals/jama/fullarticle/2771764`.

8. Jennifer Abbasi, "Large Meta-analysis Digs into Obesity's COVID-19 Risks," *JAMA* 324, no. 17 (November 03, 2020): 1709–1711, https://jamanetwork.com/journals/jama/fullarticle/2772071.
9. David Quammen, "How Viruses Shape Our World," *National Geographic,* February 2021, 48.
10. Lee Simmons, "How Narcissistic Leaders Destroy from Within," Stanford Graduate School of Business, April 30, 2020, https://stanford.io/3f4169L.

3 Swarming Simplicity

I think the next century will be the century of complexity.
—Stephen Hawking

On October 16, 2019, a newly hired young Microsoft software engineer named Michael Bervell typed up an invitation to a scavenged email list of fellow early-in-career (EIC) newbies like himself at the big tech company. "I am piloting a program called Growth Groups and wanted to see if you were interested in joining one! 'Growth Groups' are a way for EIC Microsoft hires to develop professionally alongside and create friendships with other EIC hires." He included a bit more information and welcomed people to email him back. He hoped to get 20 people, maybe 25. He received enthusiastic responses from 96. In an attempt to orient himself to his professional landscape and find some new friends, Michael Bervell had just launched an epidemic in one of the world's biggest and most established tech companies.

How Do They Do It?

As defined by Merriam-Webster, *epidemic* is "an outbreak of disease that spreads quickly and affects many individuals at the same time: an outbreak of epidemic disease." The same source defines *pandemic* as "an outbreak of a disease that occurs over a wide geographic area (such as multiple countries or continents) and typically affects a significant proportion of the population: a pandemic outbreak of a disease." The definitions don't mention leading, following, or organizing. Nonetheless, the features of an epidemic listed in Chapter 2—exponential growth, self-organization, efficient use of host resources, using available resources rather than extra ones, adaptation, self-organization, distributed intelligence, success in duress, and a hedge against destructive egos—would seem to be fine work for any leader. In fact, our leadership and business vocabulary comprises a list of almost epidemic-like words: agile, adaptable, sustainable, innovative, resilient.

We use such words to define the impact of effective leadership and organization, but epidemics seem to be better at delivering on them. If we were to stack COVID-19 against all the leadership capacity in the world contesting it in 2020, we would have to say COVID got the better of efforts to stop it. The pandemic was agile and ascendant, popping up over here whenever we thought we had it held down over there. It showed up on every continent, reemerged where it had been tamped down, and kept showing up where it had not yet been, even reaching Antarctica by December of 2020.[1] The virus was adaptive as well, mutating multiple times and making itself more infectious. After jumping, presumably, from an uncertain animal host to humans, it jumped from humans back to other animals. It overwhelmed mink farms worldwide and even showed up in pets and zoo animals. Against our dollars, our communication networks, and our impressive cognitive intelligence, this brainless phenomenon didn't just sustain itself, it expanded, and its presence among us went from "suddenly here" to "new abnormal" and probably to "here forever."

On the leadership side, with all our intent to communicate clearly, get people on the same page, respond collectively with common-sense behavior, or create a robust testing strategy and capacity, we were not able to do so. We had elaborate transportation networks, communication networks, social networks—it flowed through all of them. In the face of hundreds of thousands of deaths, the graphic suffering, the economic urgency, and the constant chatter about the virus itself, we could not organize against it as well as it organized within and among us.

The exception would be in the worldwide shared work of creating multiple highly effective vaccines. My medical electronic channels were alive early with information about and invitation to collaborative innovation around developing vaccines and sharing knowledge, learning, and challenges. We humans created several vaccines at a record pace, although that work quickly collided with distribution challenges and hesitation about even taking the vaccine, even on the part of health care personnel. From a leadership perspective and assuming COVID versus humans was a team sport, we might well have scored it COVID-19 1, Humans 0. Not a good start at a time when more epidemics are supposed to be on the way and COVID, far from being a hoax, was just roaring back with new adjustments of its own in the form of viral mutations that made it both more infectious and more resistant to our new vaccines.

Epidemics are doing just fine these days, and if the experts are right, their time is still coming. They are certainly passing the eye test. COVID racked up its own impressive stats, of course, but other epidemics continued moving or popped up. Over 81,000 people died of drug overdoses in the 12-month period ending in May 2020, the highest 12-month total ever.[2] After the 2020 US presidential election, millions of otherwise rational people infected each other with a perceptual virus called "Stop the Steal," convinced against reality that the presidential election had been fraudulent despite the overwhelming evidence to the contrary. In Georgia, we saw two notable epidemics going in different directions in the same state circumstances. The Stop-the-Steal epidemic postelection was one, but a quieter one started in South Carolina by the women of the WNBA basketball team Atlanta Dream was simple and impactful. "Vote Warnock" catapulted Raphael Warnock from single-digit polling numbers as late as August 2020 into a successful runoff position after the November election and ultimately to a seat in the US Senate as the first Black senator from his state in history. In Australia, a doctor named Catherine Barrett convened The Kindness Epidemic to help people whose lives were affected by COVID. It swelled to over 550,000 people in two weeks.

What kind of wacky world are we living in these days? Should we shrug with fatalism or pay attention with curiosity to these spreading, sprawling, what-the-heck-just-happened swarming things we call epidemics? What do epidemics "know" about the world we're living in that leaders might want to think about? Why are they so successful?

The Challenge of Complexity

The world certainly seems wacky these days. We've even given it an acronym: VUCA. VUCA stands for volatile, uncertain, complex, and ambiguous. As an acronym, it arose out of the Army War College to describe the world the military had to respond in and to after the Cold War. The term helped the military move from "old rules" of military engagement to the "new rules" of modern defense and warfare. There's quite a bit written about VUCA these days, and futurist Robert Johansen even created a "VUCA prime" as an aspirational complement to the more sobering namesakes of the original VUCA. In his version, VUCA stands for visionary, understanding, clarity, and agility.[3]

On top of VUCA, we might add high-velocity. By both objective and subjective measures, we find ourselves sped up in a world where the pace and volume of information itself is overwhelming, compounding the odds of locking ourselves into old patterns at the very time we are trumpeting the need for new ones. As a smattering of the endless statistics one can find about technology use alone, consider the following on the Vermont.gov website as a caution for those who would drive without discontinuing their steady stream of texting:[4]

- The number of monthly texts sent increased more than 7,700% over the last decade. (Statistic Brain)
- Over 560 billion texts are sent every month worldwide. (Statistic Brain) (Tweet this!)

- 18.7 billion texts are sent worldwide every day, not including app-to-app messaging. (Statistic Brain)
- (2017 Update) 15,220,700 texts are sent every minute of every day worldwide, not including app-to-app messaging. (Domo)

For a more immediate perspective, watch a video ad on the web or television and count the images per commercial.

In this ocean of "hyperpace," what to do next, how to do it, and why to do it can paralyze leaders, organizations, and teams or send us scurrying with emphatic determination to ply methods that just don't work very well. Microprocessing may follow Moore's law, which says that processing speed will double every 18 months, but the human brain does not follow Moore's law. (It turns out Moore's law itself may be coming to an end after all, according to an article in *MIT Technology Review*.[5]) In fact, the faster our brains go, the more they follow old patterns and become entrenched and reactive—less and less able to respond with new approaches in a world quickly orbiting toward new requirements. Our brains need slow time.

It's Not Just Complicated

Whatever terms we use, these days, the world is not merely complicated, it's complex. *Roget's Thesaurus* considers the two words synonyms, but (apologies to Roget and his descendant editors) they are not the same. Complicated refers to challenges and obstacles that can be solved with a known and repeatable series of steps. Complicated problems have traceable causes, connections, and results. With enough diligence, we can reduce "complicated" to static patterns and relationships. Bewildering they may seem at first, but we can solve them with perseverance, repetition, quality control, recipes, and protocols. You can figure complicated out. Putting together a model car or rocket can be complicated; the mechanical infrastructure in a house or a high-rise can be complicated. There's an answer. And it's right or it's wrong, even if there are multiple answers. Once you've figured it out, you can repeat it a thousand times.

Complexity doesn't work that way.

Complexity replaces the elaborate ordering of a more static universe with the presence of intersecting variables whose patterns of interactions are themselves variable, unpredictable in any moment, and constantly influencing each other in ways both observable and unobservable. In other words, we can't really understand a system completely and definitively in real time—it keeps surprising us. Looking back, we can see patterns; looking forward, we can try to make predictions, but surprises will always pop up, and long-range prediction and accuracy is very difficult. Planning becomes far less effective in complex environments than sensing, responding, adapting.

The Heisenberg uncertainty principle in physics is a classic observation about a complex system: we can know the location of an electron or its velocity, but not both. Volatility, uncertainty, and ambiguity can be found in spades in complex settings, as can things that appear entirely at odds, coexisting together. In complexity, you can find order and chaos, stability, and instability. Actions create the proverbial intended and unintended effects. Complexity *cannot* be broken down into linear, predictable patterns of cause and effect. The mixing of genes in a population in a variable environment is complex. The dynamics of climate change are complex, as are the results of responsive action to climate. Stopping opioids is complex. How an organization thinks and acts as a summation of how everyone in that organization thinks and acts is complex, which is why "culture eats strategy for lunch."

The difference between complicated and complex would be a boring conceptual distinction (which may be why Roget just doesn't bother!) except for this dilemma: if you try to solve complexity by the same approach you would take to address complicated, you make it worse, not better. Rick Nason, a professor of finance at Dalhoussie University's Rowe School of Business, makes this point exactly in his book *It's Not Complicated*. Complexity and complication require different approaches. What works in one setting does not work in the other. Building solutions in complicated scenarios requires analytical iteration and deductive thinking to solve. It's like putting together a large puzzle with a lot of pieces. It may be difficult, but there's an order, and there's a finite and definitive assembly. The puzzle is done, and all the pieces are in place.

Complexity is messier. Being meticulous, organized, and deductive doesn't necessarily get you where you want to go. In complexity, we tend to see some interesting things. There are multiple variables, interacting in ways that are difficult to discern in real time and in linear cause-effect terms. Relationships between objects and groups of objects tend to be interdependent, not independent; behavior is correspondingly semi-autonomous. Things behave in ways that are both independent *and* simultaneously connected. Pairings of apparent opposites crop up. Order and disorder are linked. Stability and instability can occur simultaneously. Some things are getting bigger while others are getting smaller. These pairings are not opposites so much as complements, and the universe is full of them. Consider how the universe is expanding while stars are contracting under their own gravity and mass.

Complicated we know how to solve. Complexity requires a different toolbox.

You can't "solve" complexity. It's more like the atmosphere we live in. It's a condition, not a solvable problem. It "solves itself" via things called "complex adaptive systems"—webs of relationships and participating elements whose constant, stabilizing adaptation stem from almost magical qualities: *fundamental simplicity, self-organization, and emergence*. There are complexity scientists and theorists who can go into these things in far greater detail, via mathematical equations on nonlinear dynamics and with terms such as *fractal, disentanglement,* and *semi-autonomy*. Beyond the theoretical exploration of complexity is our practical goal of reflecting on epidemics as successful manifestations of leading in our complex times and environment.

The Power of Simplicity

You wouldn't think simplicity would underlie complexity, but handily for us, it does. At the root of unbelievably complex systems are very simple foundational elements. Powerful computer simulations have modeled complex order from such simple subunits.[6] More intuitively, we can recognize that just as an endless beach is clearly made of small grains of sand, complex systems like our bodies are made up of much smaller and more simple subunits called cells, and that a large block of salt is made up of tiny, cube-shaped crystals of sodium chloride.

Further, those self-repeating but ever bigger or smaller blocks of salt are made up of smaller particles we know as atoms, but always equal portions of sodium and chloride, and only sodium and chloride.

The Miracle of Self-Organization

Self-organization seems a particularly bizarre concept in a universe in which entropy is at play, but it happens all the time. Salt is again a great example. Put a bunch of sodium and chloride in water, and you'll have a bunch of sodium ions, which have a positive charge, bobbing around with a bunch of chloride ions, which have a negative charge. Now let the water stand in the sun and evaporate. The sodium and chloride will always organize themselves into sheets and stacks of minicubes—never hexagons, never octagons. Never! Snowflakes are another example, with the unique flair that every snowflake is a different riff on a universal theme. Let water condense in the cold and fall out of the sky, and crystalline snowflakes fall out every time, each one exquisitely symmetric and ornate. Snowflakes are *always* hexagonal, with six sides and not five or seven—but never *exactly* the same shape. This pattern-making function continues and manifests itself in the form of networks. In the body, stem cells organize into tubular structures we call blood vessels, and these then organize into a network of bifurcating vasculature that allows our heart to deliver and retrieve nutrition and waste to and from every one of our 300 trillion cells. No manual, no quickstart guide. It just happens, almost every time.

Popping Up When We Least Expect It

Emergence is the property we call "*greater than the sum of its parts.*" In emergence, things go into motion, and despite the fact that you think you've identified all the reality inherent in the parts themselves, something else "pops up." You can't tell *what* is going to pop up (can you ever, in life, as much as we forget that it's true?!), but you can be sure *things will,* no matter how hard and how well you *plan*. Consciousness is an example. Each of us has a nervous system with 100 billion cells. They are all linked together into an elaborate, tangled raft and fire off signals to each other. We can track the signals in intensity and flow, we can discern definite tracts of signal flow, and we know much about how they work at the molecular level. We know what the cells are made of, we know what's in them, how they transport ions across their cell membranes as they talk to each other, but we *cannot* explain how what amounts to a low-level electrical cloud of static creates thoughts like, "Wow, what a beautiful sunset," or "It is inspiring to watch those people dance," or "My uncle's armpits just don't smell good."

You don't have to be a complexity scientist to observe that our world is full of complex adaptive systems where simplicity riffs into self-organized emergence. Societies, economies, and galaxies all exhibit complex, adaptive activity. Ant colonies and human bodies are complex adaptive systems and are complex adaptive subsystems of the overarching complex adaptive system of biological life itself. We are so familiar with this web of life and living that we often take it for granted at numerous levels, but no other system remotely like it exists in our knowable exploration of the entire universe.

We have tangible experiences that make these phenomena accessible to us at a personal level. Ask anyone about their best team experience, and they will begin to describe a favorite memory as a complex adaptive system: "things took on a life of their own," "we were all responding to each other, but no one was coercing anyone," "things happened that I never would have guessed we could do," and "we were more than the sum of our parts." People will describe adaptation: "we changed the plan right then and there, and then we changed it again when this or that happened." They'll describe emergence: "the whole is greater than the sum of its parts," or "after we did this and that, an entirely new reality appeared." They'll also describe self-organization: "even though we all had our formal roles, we were re-organizing on the fly so things worked better, and there wasn't any arguing." These are peak experiences for many, and they can relate the story of what happened and what it felt like vividly many years later.

Is Complexity a New "Thing"?

Do we *really* live in a different world today? Yes and no. The planet Earth has always been a complex adaptive system and part of the larger complex system of the universe. The interplay between gravity, atmosphere, incoming energy from the sun; the collision and combination of atoms and molecules and their organization into geology and biology; the unfolding of simple and elegant elements into infinitely complex creatures, populations, and ecosystems boggles the mind with regard to how it happens, where it came from, why it's here, where it's going.

That said, we humans have clearly created a society where things are even more complex. We are not just sitting in the world or looking at it; we are part of it. Accordingly the complexity we've added is consistent with complexity itself begetting more complexity (and new order). For people who like new things, unpredictability, and infinite possibilities, this age is a fun time to be alive. For those who prefer the way things were, predictability, and known realities, this age can be frightening indeed.

Our technology platforms, transportation connectivity, long supply chains, multiple languages and frames of reference, our economies and institutions, and the size and diversity of our population have all introduced multiple intersecting variables into a world in which complexity was already waiting for us. Finally, our collective *awareness* of this complexity has hit home. We're noticing complexity more—or at least its effects—at work, at home, and in institutions. It has been building for years, but COVID-19 has been a shattering and grounding event. As my colleague Michael Wagner, MD, says about the COVID-19 spectrum of effects: "The world will be forever changed, as will many leaders."

We are no longer assuming stability; we no longer assume our institutions will hum along in the background; we no longer assume our health; we no longer assume toilet paper will be right around the corner. To be sure, many saw this non-negotiable reckoning with complexity coming, and marginalized people have experienced instability, poverty, household economic volatility, and institutional ambiguity for generations, but at this moment in our history, huge portions of people in old and new categories are realizing, in whatever way they say it to themselves or their friends: *this is not working anymore*. Leaders are often the last to say this, conspired as we are to inspire (we tend to leave the bad news to the heretics and the skeptics), but the time is here. What we're doing is not matching the challenges at hand. We can do better.

What Does Leading Look Like in Complexity?

I've heard very emphatic people argue back and forth about this question without resolution. I've heard some say leadership is more important than ever, while others say complexity renders leadership meaningless and unnecessary, an anachronistic and complicating attempt to force order. A clue to the value of leadership in complex environments becomes apparent in the design of complex systems themselves. Complex adaptive systems seem to find their capacity in the quality and design of their relationships, not in the primacy of any particular sub-element. After all, any neuron among your 100 billion nerve cells, or any of your 100 trillion cells, could disappear, and you wouldn't miss a beat. Leadership as an individual point source seems an almost quaint notion in a complex adaptive system. Which is the alpha elk in a vast species? Which coronavirus particle influences the others?

Amid complexity, the traditional leadership focus on skills in individual leaders, even when those skills are designed to create effects across wide spans of influence, seems underpowered in the face of what complexity throws at us. The noted systems scientist Peter Senge puts it this way:

> *Our traditional view of leaders—as special people who set the direction, make the key decisions and energize the troops—is deeply rooted in an individualistic and non-systemic worldview. So long as such myths prevail, they reinforce a focus on short-term events and charismatic heroes rather than on systemic forces and collective learning.*[7]

Conventional approaches tap the authority and influence of a particular leader (or group of leaders) and translate that social power across processes and rules in settings where relatively few people hold social power. In essence, leadership has been about positioning single leaders as point sources who can cast their personal influence and authority across a defined envelope of activity. Such an approach can be done well or poorly with respect to serving and listening to followers or manipulating and directing them. Such an approach is not incorrect so much as it is inadequate to meet all the challenges coming at us. In the multivariate world of complexity, where problems and answers can originate and flourish from any point and angle, such point-source leadership cannot match the capacity and pace of the problems we are encountering.

We know that leaders who can lead in complexity create tangible, rare value. Consider that companies with complexity-comfortable leaders are *three times more likely* to be in the top quintile of financial performance than their competitors without such leaders.[8] Oddly, in my many years of leadership training, I have heard a lot about the *need* for leaders to lead in complexity, but I heard precious little about *how* to do it, and most of what I did had to do with avoiding being complicated (which is always worth remembering). I often learned more working with my horses or listening to how assembled groups figured something out very quickly and well. Whatever it looks like, leading in complexity is a worthwhile skill, and with all this complexity flying around, now appears to be the time. These days, there is an increasing body of work defining how leadership can think and act in complex environments.

In the years since my epidemic anti-epiphany in the ER and its sleep-deprived crystallization that biology works by better rules, I had continued to think about what leadership really does. There are endless definitions of leadership, of course. One of the ones I like best is from the Center for Creative Leadership: DAC. The acronym stands for direction, alignment, and commitment.[9] How you get that done is a matter of style, competency, and strategy. The three words strike me as tacking to a social physics of sorts. Organize particles (called people) so they move in the same direction, so they move smoothly without crashing harmfully into each other or opposing each other, and somehow get them to pour more energy into the action than the friction or resistance the obstacles and challenges are meting out. It's tidy. It's Newtonian. It's not wrong, and it describes what happens.

That definition says nothing, though, about helping life do what it does. All living things embody the defining properties of life that we learn about in grade school, high school, college, or beyond, depending on our depth of exposure. Every grade school biology classroom has a poster hanging on the wall with the defining characteristics of life. Those defining properties include a cell-based structure, growth, reproduction, adaptation, homeostasis (maintenance of life processes), use of energy, and response to the environment.[10]

At one level, these concepts are powerful metaphor for any leader or business who hopes to create widespread, sustained function: what is the "cell" of your business, how does it homeostase, or stabilize, its business processes, how does it respond to market environments, and so forth.

On the other hand, these concepts are not metaphor but literal reality. Leaders, teams, companies, and institutions are not *like* living systems; human organizations *are* living systems—made up of living things called people.

Biology's Answer to Leading: PLV

All living things have to *perform*. If not, they're "out of the system," that is, they're dead. We can define performance—and generate data on it—in limitless ways, but if organisms perform, they get to hang around, and if they don't, that is, by definition, the end of surviving. Further, they don't survive–perform in a static environment. Every day is different, with new challenges, new opportunities. Environmental conditions change, competitors and collaborators come and go. If organisms and populations do not adjust, they cannot perform, and they cannot survive. These adjustments are really *learning*, and they have to be constant and iterative to match conditions. If an organism or population cannot learn, it also cannot perform, and it cannot survive. In order to be able to adjust to the constant changes inevitable in any external environment, to keep learning amid the unpredictabilities of a complex world, living things have to be *vital*. They have to be metabolically rigorous, capable of sustaining themselves, and creating subsequent life behind them. If your vitality is zero, you're already dead, but if your vitality is insufficient to support the necessary learning and performance, it is only a matter of time before you are.

I have started calling these things PLV—performance, learning, and vitality. Biology is unequivocal on all three of these points. No performance, you die. No learning, you die as soon as change requires adjustment and you can't make the adjustment (which is always soon). No vitality; you can't learn or perform, so you will die, or you are already dead. We humans have to do the same thing. We have to create PLV.

We call performance by other names, of course: *results, metrics, OKRs, KPIs*. We have names for learning also: *training, information transfer, development, adaptation, agility, innovation, change management*. We also have vitality, which we name by its opposites—*burnout, exhaustion, apathy*—as well as its surrogates: *engagement, commitment, well-being, wellness, commitment, sustainability*. In biology, PLV domains are not distinct and separate, they are integral and inseparable. A cheetah cannot perform without learning, cannot learn without being vital; neither can bacteria, ants, or horses. We can define performance, learning, and vitality in uncountable ways, but if an organism or population isn't exhibiting all three, it is in trouble and at risk.

In biology, and accordingly in all biological things, PLV is what complexity scientists call a fractal. A fractal is a self-repeating unit that holds at different scales. The fractal in our vascular system is the bifurcated blood vessel. Your aorta forks into two main vessels, the iliacs, in your abdomen, and then those fork and so on, and so on. The forking has different calibers or diameters, but the arterial and venous arcades of your body are links of forks.

PLV is a fractal in our bodies and in our organizations. Cells have to PLV, tissues have to PLV, organs have to PLV, and humans as whole organisms have to PLV. Individuals in a team have to PLV in their roles; teams have to PLV in their function, and so forth. We can and should define what sort of PLV is required from each of our constituents in social organizations, but the rule holds: no PLV, no good. If a part of a living whole is not embodying PLV, the part is either superfluous or creating risk.

Further, biology has to scale PLV across all the cells in a particular body and across populations and ecosystems. It doesn't do any good for 20 percent of an organism's cells to be sailing along with robust PLV while 80 percent of them are not; the same holds for any population. Biology scales via the linked patterns and networks that define biological structure—both via structural networks, like grass and tree roots and blood vessels and genetic trees, and also via relational networks like the ones we see in elephant herds, beehives, and human teams. Whether you are a shrew or a fungus, a bacterium or a hippopotamus, these processes are fundamentally universal.

The biological deliverable of leadership, then, is the scaling of PLV among followers and participants into viable and sustainable individuals, populations, and ecosystems.

On this planet, biology is the operating system. It's not "*an* operating system"; it's *the* operating system. Not some places and not others. Everywhere. Our politics, our economies, our neighborhoods, our cities, our commerce and industry, our art and language, are all expressions of biology.

From it, to us, around us, through us, and from us, biology creates and scales all patterns of PLV. As biological creatures living, relating, and creating their own individual and shared PLV in biological communities we call teams, companies, neighborhoods, and institutions, leaders have to work with many topics, people, timeframes, and dynamics, so PLV once, or even on occasion, isn't sufficient, any more than it is for a horse or an ant to embody PLV once and then take the rest of life off. Leaders have to scale and sustain PLV.

How Are Epidemics and Leaders Doing in Complexity?

We may not like COVID-19's embodiment of PLV, but it scaled across our patterns and created new ones. It multiplied the number of infections, spread against resistance, killed people, commanded unbelievable amounts of countering resource, and moved faster than we could stop it. It checked the box for P = Performance. It mutated and leaped from species to species, wormed its way into new networks, became more infectious, began mutating toward vaccine resistance. It checked the box for L = Learning. As for V = Vitality, the pandemic exhausted us psychically, operationally, civically, and for many physically (and worse, terminally or permanently), but the pandemic itself showed sustainable staying power. It did not tire, and individual coronavirus particles were not "red-lining" to get through their days or make all their calendar appointments. It checked the box for V = Vitality. It started with a single case and escalated into the millions. COVID checked the S = Scale box.

How Leaders Do in Complexity

I hear from a lot of leaders. Both the conversations and the data suggest we are at a PLV deficit relative to the number of things being asked of leaders these days. Scale is a constant problem, as is sustainability. "Do it yourself," or "The minute we turn our head, things lapse back" are both common themes, as are "too much to do, not enough time." Leaders, followers, companies, and entire sectors and communities are facing the PLV deficit right now.

Our traditional response to this "trilemma" has been to go harder, work longer, and short-change the regeneration of our physical, emotional, and spiritual energy. The data would suggest this heroic approach is not going so well: more people are feeling burned out than before the pandemic, and two thirds of people think burnout has worsened.[11,12] More quietly, I hear from larger numbers of very successful people who say, quietly and honestly, "I just can't do this anymore." Leaders also have to lead in a world where individuals feel increasingly small, insignificant, and unheard, where we are indentured by debt, the hyperpace of daily tasks, and technological platforms that keep us numbingly scrolling and clicking along.

Epidemics Invite a New Framework

In complexity terms, we could define epidemics as biological phenomena that scale adaptive PLV by leveraging patterns of action and interaction in populations, which are themselves networks. Their continued interactions drive constant and relentless adaptability, resilience, and emergence of new realities. COVID-19, like all epidemics, is a complex adaptive phenomenon perfectly tailored to arise and thrive in the larger complex system of life on Earth. In the sense that it's creating PLV—admittedly not *our* version—it is showing us what leadership looks like in complex environments. Epidemics invite us to think of leadership as creating agile, responsive, human-technology communities and networks where more effective patterns of thought and action are infectious. Easily picked up, easily passed.

Epidemic leadership can now be defined in human systems: the intentional scaling of PLV by shifting patterns of thought (because we have brains), action, and interaction within populations and networks. PLV forever, across any and all topics in whatever circumstances, is leadership's job. Simple. Not easy.

There's a wonderful take-home here for leaders. If we're living in a complex world, where widespread PLV is a requisite survival capacity and where scaling that triad creates profound capacity, complexity becomes your ally and greatest leverage if you know how to use it. Epidemics can show us how. Viewed against dimensions of complexity, the success of epidemics in complex environments becomes clear, and they begin to define a blueprint for leading in complex environments. They offer a path to PLV at scale and powerful clues to how to shift patterns of thought, action, and interaction in networks.

In complex environments, leading and designing from simplicity is not just a shortcut hack, it is the *ideal* way to build in adaptability in anticipation of certain but unpredictable challenges. You *do not* have to have every competency; your job is to create capacity within the networks and population. You don't have to start over and reinvent yourself; you just have to facilitate how the assets in your human system multiply and (self-)organize.

You could also take the complicated route. You can try to solve for every outcome and try to cut complexity off at the pass with protocols, processes, and elimination of variability. In a world where we have been indoctrinated within the Cartesian boundaries of spreadsheets and rectangles, rules and policies, it is a tempting and oft-practiced approach. It won't work. The nature of a complex world dictates that a complicated approach will leave you with too much to do, not enough time to do it, and not enough energy to keep going. Smart calendaring will not solve this problem.

Key Questions for Leaders

Epidemics certainly confront us with some sticky questions. As I have listened to leaders exploring the idea of leading like an epidemic, they have raised numerous questions that speak to the tension between conventional and complexity approaches to leadership.

- Is leading exponentially some sort of Orwellian mass manipulation, or can it be widely volitional and participative and still be effective, coherent, and directional?
- Does creating collective intelligence undermine the idea of an individual's unique contributions?
- If epidemic approaches democratize leadership, what does that say about how different people lead differently (and better or worse)? Do epidemics assume leadership relativism? If we go multipoint source from a leadership perspective, aren't we democratizing chaos, not leadership?
- Is "overwhelmed and behind" just the way of the world? Is the quest to perform and survive in a world where change comes so fast from so many directions always going to trump the need and right for vitality and well-being?

The questions are personal as well as conceptual.

- Am I ready to embrace ideas like self-organization, emergence, and epidemic design to lead exponentially?
- Is what I learned about leadership outdated and irrelevant?
- Do I have to think and act differently to get things done?

In his 2014 book *Accelerate*, John Kotter, the author of numerous books on change, posited that organizations need two operating systems. One is formal, top-down, and hierarchical, designed to maintain stability and continue rote processes that are beneficial. The other is looser, more horizontal, less formal, and designed to surface new ideas, entrepreneurial thinking, and innovation, "more like a start-up's solar system than a mature organization's Giza pyramid."

Healthy organizations need both these capabilities, of course, and there is value in both approaches.

What you've learned to date about leading and leadership is certainly valuable. Your leadership toolbox and mental model is full of things that biology insists on continuously: things to keep and hold, things to discard and slough off, and new things to bring in and learn.

Epidemic leadership should not replace everything you've learned; it can add on to your worthy efforts. You do not have to change—you get to decide. Epidemic action is already at play in your system, usually to your disadvantage. I have seen leaders put this kind of approach to work with great success and very little resistance, and I also had a couple of my own executive team members leave as a result of it, off to environments where the thinking was more conventional and to their liking.

The Math Problem Leaders Face

A decade before Michael Bervell sent out his initial email, I walked into our executive meeting early in my tenure at Memorial Health System.

Heads were down, calculators were out, and spreadsheets sprawled across the large table where we met. No one looked up as I entered. I watched for a few moments and then interrupted them.

"Hi. What are you all doing?"

They glanced up, eyebrows raised. "Working. It's a long list."

"That's an interesting point," I said. "How long *is* the list?"

"Really long. Too long." Their attention lapsed back into their work.

"Seriously, let's count out the lists. Let's add 'em up." We went around the room, with each executive listing the things on his or her list. The total, as I recall, was north of 230.

"Okay, how many things will you cross off by the end of the day?"

"You mean, all the way off, as in 'done'?"

"Let's say done enough to know that in a couple or three days, they'll be off your plate." We totaled again. The number was 13.

"Ok, how many *new* things will be on each of your lists by the end of the day?"

Two or three of them nodded. The others looked at me, blinking. "We have a math problem," one of them said. "We're just going to get farther behind."

"I'm wondering what the connection is between this long list and my made-up disease of Chronic Proliferative Dysphoria."

"I think it's all about accountability," the Chief Nursing Officer piped up. "I want to know who's going to keep people accountable. It has to be us. You can't just keep people happy."

"Agreed—we certainly have to be accountable to the performance of this organization, to its ability to learn and adjust and adapt in a thousand ways. And we have to be accountable to the vitality of this place and its work, its people. The question is, 'How?'"

Our CMIO spoke. He was an emergency physician, and he would shortly be charged with the thankless job of getting his physician colleagues to adopt the use of an electronic medical record they had rejected on its first attempted implementation. The doctors experienced the computerized record as a surefire way to slow patient flow and increase safety risk in the ED. They refused to leave paper charts. Looking at his executive teammates, he asked, "Who keeps me accountable in the emergency department in the middle of the night?"

"I assume it's your department chair and the policies of the hospital, maybe the department of medical examiners," replied one.

"No, it's not. I hope those things are helpful, but it's really me, my teammates, and the patient in front of me. That's where accountability comes from when no one's looking. And we need that everywhere. There are more times when no one's looking than when someone is."

In a few sentences, he had drawn out our shared leadership challenge: to chase after PLV by what we proclaimed and codified or to grow it by how we interacted and related. At that moment, we could have embarked on an epidemic of accountability. We chose a different epidemic, though. We created a lot of accountability along the way, but I think if we had started with an epidemic named accountability, we might not have ended up where we did.

Notes

1. Brakkton Booker, "The Coronavirus Has Reached Antarctica. Now It's on Every Continent," NPR, December 23, 2020, https://www.npr.org/sections/coronavirus-live-updates/2020/12/23/949552848/the-coronavirus-has-reached-every-continent-after-positive-cases-in-antarctica.
2. "Overdose Deaths Accelerating During COVID-19: Expanded Prevention Efforts Needed," Centers for Disease Control and Prevention, last reviewed December 18, 2020, https://www.cdc.gov/media/releases/2020/p1218-overdose-deaths-covid-19.html.
3. Leading Effectively Staff, "Leadership Skills in an Uncertain World," Center for Creative Leadership, November 11, 2020, https://www.ccl.org/articles/leading-effectively-articles/leadership-skills-for-an-uncertain-world/.

4. "Worldwide Testing Statistics," https://shso.vermont.gov/sites/ghsp/files/documents/Worldwide%20Texting%20Statistics.pdf.
5. David Rotman, "We're Not Prepared for the End of Moore's Law," *MIT Technology Review*, February 24, 2020, https://www.technologyreview.com/2020/02/24/905789/were-not-prepared-for-the-end-of-moores-law/.
6. Geoffrey West, *Scale: The Universal Laws of Growth, Innovation, Sustainability, and the Pace of Life in Organisms, Cities, Economies, and Companies* (New York: Penguin Press, 2017), 22.
7. Peter Senge, "The Leader's New Work: Building Learning Organizations," *Sloan Management Review*, Fall 1990, 7–23.
8. "Eight Critical Capabilities for a Complex World," Harvard Business Publishing Corporate Learning, 2018, https://2uzkee3eob510v4rszskfx11-wpengine.netdna-ssl.com/wp-content/uploads/2018/11/8CriticalCapabilities_Nov2018.pdf.
9. Wilfred H. Drath et al., "Direction, Alignment, Commitment: Toward a More Integrative Ontology of Leadership," *The Leadership Quarterly* 19, no. 6 (December 2008): 636–637, https://doi.org/10.1016/j.leaqua.2008.09.003.
10. "What Are the Characteristics of Living Things?" Reference.com, updated March 25, 2020, https://www.reference.com/science/characteristics-living-things-d5fc0441ef59f417.
11. Kristy Threlkeld, "Employee Burnout Report: COVID-19's Impact and 3 Strategies to Curb It," Indeed.com, March 11, 2021, https://www.indeed.com/lead/preventing-employee-burnout-report.
12. Jack Kelly, "Indeed Study Shows That Worker Burnout Is at Frighteningly High Levels: Here Is What You Need to Do Now," *Forbes*, April 5, 2021, https://www.forbes.com/sites/jackkelly/2021/04/05/indeed-study-shows-that-worker-burnout-is-at-frighteningly-high-levels-here-is-what-you-need-to-do-now/?sh=1429622023bb.

4 Something from Nothing

Simple clear purpose and principles give rise to complex, intelligent behavior. Complex rules and regulations give rise to simple, stupid behavior.

—Dee Hock, Chairman Emeritus, VISA International

In the Shade of the Mango Tree

March 2018, Masese Town, Jinja District, Uganda

I am standing under a big mango tree with 25 teachers and staff at the HELP primary school. The two-acre schoolyard is orange dust, an old brick foundry now enclosed by high brown brick walls with an iron gate. Outside, the dirt streets run with sewage and swirl with trash. Toddlers, chickens, and goats sift through a smoldering pile of it. Dilapidated makeshift buildings line the smelly streets like derailed miniature train cars. Inside, the sounds and smells beyond the walls are muted. Thirty staff and teachers and I are standing in loose pairs encircled by chairs in the shade of the old tree, sipping Fanta and Mirinda sodas.

I had just asked the school staff a couple of questions about their students as a group. They switched in and out of conversing pairs, listening to one another's observations of the students. The first question was what they saw in the students as reservoirs of hope for a vibrant future. The second was what was missing. Language was hard, my American accent clashing on their Ugandan ears. Although English is the official language of Uganda, many find it easier to speak in one or more native Ugandan tongues. My friend Frederick, on the leadership team of the school and a pastor in a local church, translated for me, ferrying words and insights back and forth.

"What did you hear from each other?" I asked.

"Our children have dreams," they said. "They work hard. They do not want to live in poverty. They want to build a beautiful future for Masese."

"What is missing in them?" I looked from pair to pair. Eyes looked back, knowing. No one said anything. "It can be hard to say what we see sometimes. What would you give to these children if you could, so their dreams could flourish?"

"They are used to having nothing; they don't know anything else. So when something bad happens, they do not think trying more will be of any use . . ." "They are used to it. They don't know how to keep going, to not give up . . ." "They don't think dreams are real. They don't think they can make a dream come true."

I listened to the run of responses coming in English and languages I didn't understand, translated through Frederick. I thought of the children I saw playing at recess and working in the crowded mudbrick classrooms. They ran and jumped and played like children who had a future, but the teachers knew that belief was fragile. Several of the teachers had brought me to their classrooms, and the beginning was always tellingly formulaic.

"Students, this is Dr. Larry. Please say hello."

"Hello, Dr. Larry!"

"Hello, everyone. How are you?"

"Good! We are humble and obedient." Every time. Huge smiles and the same words.

My attention tumbled back into the circle. It had gone silent. We had gotten to the core of the reason my friend Jean-Kaye Wilson had invited me to the school. After 10 years of working to create a place where these children could attend a school with a stable environment and succeed at primary education, she, the board, the staff, the students, and the families were at an impasse. The students were working; they were getting good scores. In the old British system of education that held sway in the school, they were drilled and drilled until they remembered. They were poised to move on, but there was so much more in their way—generations of trauma from civil war, resource degradation, 80 percent unemployment, corruption. These weren't issues. They weren't topics or nuance. They were permeating, defining reality.

"What I hear you saying," I started, "was that they don't know how to make something from nothing." The pairs nodded quietly. "And they need to know how to do that."

"Only God can do that."

We all laughed.

In the pause that followed, a young woman spoke. "We don't know how to do that, either. If we are going to show them, we are going to have to learn for ourselves."

"It is what you are wanting these kids to do." The enormity of it hung in us all, palpable over the dust we were standing in. I felt my long-lost ER-Saturday-night feeling.

"When you introduce me to the students, what do they say when I ask how they are?"

"They say they are humble and obedient."

"What do you think of those words?" The teachers assembled the entire school every morning for announcements, and obedience was a priority. The children responded in unison to the question that started every day, "We are humble and obedient!"

"We are proud of them. Students should be humble and obedient."

"Will those two words help them do something different?" Brows furrowed. "Can children turn dreams into reality with those two words? Are those two words enough to go from nothing to something?"

"We need a new word!" One of the teachers, known for having a quiet voice, was now emphatic and clear. "These two words keep us where we are. We need a word that moves us forward. All of us."

We ended the day there, with an agreement to meet in the circle of shade in the dust under the big mango tree the next day. Their task was to reflect on a word that could move everyone in the school, in every subject and activity. I was off to listen to the older students about their dreams.

Miracle Parts

Something from nothing. It's what epidemics do, born by their ability to self-organize into rapid growth. By blossoming from tiny anonymous particles into patterns that sprawl into new reality across our social networks, they give us a map for how to go from "behind and outmatched" to "catching up and sailing past" by virtue of their exponential growth. In doing so they answer one of the profound challenges to leaders in a complex world: capacity and staying power beyond our individual efforts.

How Do They Do It?

As Dee Hock's quote in Chapter 3 about complex intelligent behavior so wonderfully captures, simple principles are better designed to deal with complexity than complicated rules. Simple elements are more fungibly flexible into the innumerable combinations and prototypes we need to figure things out in unclear settings. Any child understands this truth about Legos; with a range of small, simple parts, one can build elaborate and infinite combinations. Get complicated and all control-oriented with chaos, and you confine yourself to a narrower range of solutions that can actually fit the unpredictable circumstances at hand. I haven't asked him, but maybe Dee Hock meant, "Simple clear purpose and principles give rise to complex, intelligent behavior. *Complicated* rules and regulations give rise to simple, stupid behavior."

Epidemics come in innumerable varieties, but they all follow a kind of universal proto-design. In essence, epidemics give us a cheat code for getting things done in complex environments—such as the ones in which leaders find themselves daily. Because their design emerges out of complexity itself, we can use their cheat code to address really deep, stubborn problems with an adaptive leadership DNA complementary to more conventional approaches.

From a scientific perspective, epidemics follow the rules of biology, networks, and complex phenomena. Epidemics harness the patterns of action and interaction to rise and spread.

In humans, behavioral epidemics move through our patterns of thought as well as through our patterns of action and interaction and accordingly follow the principles of human neurobiology. The good news for leaders is that while the science continues to illuminate how we can lead, follow, and organize in the twenty-first century, you do not have to be deeply steeped in these scientific fields to tap the advantages of epidemic design as a leader or organizer.

Beneath all the adaptation they demonstrate, epidemics are grounded in simplicity, like all things that thrive in complexity as part of adaptive systems. The leadership leverage of epidemics lies in being able to tap that simplicity to build the capacity for Dee Hock's "complex, intelligent behavior." In keeping with this theme, epidemics have three essential parts, which manifest themselves via infinite variety and combinations.

Part 1: The Pathogen

Pathogen derives from the root words *pathos*, which means "disease," and *gen*, which means "to start," or "to create." The pathogen, or "disease starter" is different from the disease itself. Ebola, the virus, locked in a freezer in a test tube somewhere, is quite harmless. It is really a glob of a DNA-like compound called RNA wrapped in proteins. In this state, it's a pathogen—something that *could cause* disease but hasn't yet; it is not self-sufficient by any means. Unless it is in a hosting system where it can multiply and create effect—a human body, for example—it's just a would-be disease, an idea. Even in that test tube, though, the essential elements of the pathogen's design encode its eventual effects as well as how it might connect to key areas of a host's metabolic workings.

Pathogens come in vast varieties and combinations. Both influenza and Ebola in a test tube are "potential diseases," for example, but the two pathogens are vastly different. Ebola holds the keys to muscle aches, fever, and internal hemorrhage by way of wrecking our clotting processes; influenza lies poised to trigger sore throat, muscle aches, pneumonia, and fevers without the dangerous bleeding. Think of the "pathogen" as the core idea, or nugget, that *could* germinate and spread into a full-blown epidemic *if* it can land in the right environment where it can multiply and spread. All epidemics are the uptake, multiplication, and spread of such a pathogen and its effects in a population. In nonliving terms, a pathogen is like a candle flame. Confined to its waxy base, it's not going anywhere. Put it on a dry forest floor when the temperature is 100 degrees Fahrenheit after three months without rain, and you've got the consumption of millions of trees and the spread of fire very quickly. The pathogen is the candle flame.

Despite the fact that a pathogen is not yet a disease but merely a "disease maker," its design is uniquely crafted to exploit opportunity when it arises. On the surface of pathogens are little protein flags or hooks called antigens that match docking receptors in the host where they will ultimately land, like a key to a lock. These receptors allow the pathogen and its docking antigens to latch onto particular cells in a host and begin to trigger specific patterns. Any behavioral pathogen, such as "collaboration" or "innovation," has to be analogously wrapped with antigenic "hooks" to allow it to stick in the mind of a waiting host if you're trying to create a social epidemic. When leaders think about the appeal of a particular idea pathogen, how they frame essential ideas becomes a valuable skill. We recognize this contextualization of ideas intuitively and call the lack of it being "tone deaf." Parents, wanting to wrap an idea in "antigens" or supporting context, can tell their young children to simply eat their peas and get over it, or they might choose helpful embellishment: "Gee, these peas are good, and just one or two of them can help you get outside to play with your friends sooner." Any given context around the idea of eating vegetables can set the stage for positive or negative response to the idea. The design of a pathogen can mean it is more easily picked up and spread down the line, both in a host and between hosts.

Coronaviruses, for example—a group that includes the COVID-19 virus, influenza viruses A and B, and the virus that causes the common cold—are exquisitely transmissible among humans, which is why COVID-19 spread so easily and persistently. HIV, on the other hand, the virus that causes AIDS, is not as transmissible. It's a dangerous virus to have in your body, but it's not as easily "picked up and passed."

Some ideas are easily picked up and passed, too; others are not. On the more difficult ones, leaders have to work harder to create an epidemic, all things being equal. Damon Centola, in his book *How Behavior Changes: The Science of Complex Contagions*, has shown that more complex behaviors require more fastidious conditions in order to move in a population. Holding a door for someone, for example, is a pathogen that spreads differently than rejecting racism. Pathogen design influences, but does not exclusively determine, the ease or difficulty of uptake and spread.

Part 2: Infection

Once a pathogen invades a host—whether by injection, inhalation, ingestion, a handshake—it has the potential to multiply. When it multiplies within a host environment, its *potential* effects can become *real* effects. For influenza, this process of multiplying within a host to cause effects means runny nose, dry burning cough, burning eyes, aching muscles, chills, and fever. All these effects totaled together are called the "disease"—the sum total of results when a pathogen multiplies within a single organism.

SARS-CoV-2, for instance, is the *pathogen* that causes COVID-19, which is the *disease* we see in people when that virus infects humans. The process of moving from "pathogen in isolation" to "effect on the host = disease" is called infection. If a pathogen can't *infect*, it can't cause disease. It can't create an effect. It's just an idea. Disease is the constellation of effects that results from a pathogen interacting with a host. Sometimes, infection takes a while to create the clinical effect of disease; this term is called latency. You might be carrying the pathogen and actively infected, but you are not yet "showing" disease. HIV is famous for having a long latency, during which time a person hosting the pathogen is infected, and contagious to others, but does not yet have the clinical manifestations of the disease AIDS.

Other times, a host can be infected but show a different range of symptoms than another host. With COVID-19, for example, one person might have been asymptomatic while another was drastically ill. Each one was infected; but one expressed clinical disease while the other did not.

Behaviorally, people can be "infected" and show "disease" in different ways as well. Two individuals can be infected with racist ideas, but one may show very little hostile behavior toward people of a different race, while another person carrying racist ideas may be more likely to graffiti racial epithets and insults on sidewalks and storefronts or participate in online hate speech. Both are infected; they express infection differently. In keeping with the dynamics of complexity, the interplay between pathogens and hosts is itself complex, which is why infectious disease shows both consistent patterns and case-to-case variability. Leaders recognize similar trends and variations within their teams, business units, and institutions, just as doctors recognize both consistent patterns and individual symptoms in their patients.

Part 3: Contagion

A pathogen simmering in one person, causing a disease or not, does not an epidemic make. Only one person is sick. For any pathogen causing a disease to grow into an epidemic, spread must happen—spread of the pathogen, spread of effects, spread of the disease. The third part of any epidemic, then, is its capacity to spread from person to person, population to population. If it can't spread, its chance for wider penetration is drastically reduced, even if infection is itself effective. There is a disease called Legionnaire's disease, originally described in Philadelphia when a convention of Legionnaires (who knew?) all got sick after they attended a convention in the same hotel. It created an outbreak—a cluster of individuals—of disease, but it never turned into an epidemic, and it still doesn't. Why? It has a nasty pathogen, a bug later named *Legionella*, and that bacterium causes a nasty-enough disease, but *Legionella* doesn't leap from person to person—you most readily contract the disease if you directly pick up the pathogen from a particular point source, water droplets from air-conditioning ducts, for example. The number of people who encounter the point source thereby limits the spread of disease. It's a hub-and-spoke model of spread. Epidemics like Ebola or influenza, or opioid use, leap from person to person and population to population. They may start as a single source, but they move quickly from single source to multisource. Think about a single drug dealer selling drugs to a group of people. If enough people in a community are using, eventually the socialization of drug use no longer depends on a single dealer or a single prescribing doctor. In the contagion of epidemics, each "host" becomes a "source" as well. COVID-19 acts this way; as soon as you have it, you can pass it on to someone else. In these cases, spread is no longer linear, and big numbers of people can become infected from small source points, particularly if those source points have a lot of nearby or frequent contacts.

Scientists spend years studying how these parts are put together and fit together. The three parts can each express themselves as countless disease phenomena. There are literally lifetimes of study spent understanding just the coronavirus family of pathogens, which represent a small part of the world of viruses, and further lifetimes exploring pathogens that are bacterial, and others that are protozoal (small animals, like the ones, for example, that cause malaria). Infection and subsequent disease, which can show up variably across different and similar hosts, is another lifetime of work. There are physician specialists in infectious disease who are experts in how pathogens infect humans, how those infections show up as patterns and iterations of clinical features, and how those diseases spread. Despite the years of impressive work that clinicians and researchers have committed to understanding, preventing, and treating these diseases, and as impressive and helpful as that knowledge is, we still have much to learn. The pathogens themselves, the processes of infection and treatment, and our understanding of contagion and how to stop it are all continued fields of study where multiple disciplines intersect. Nonetheless, if we're talking about epidemics, we're still talking about three basic parts. If an epidemic gets those three right and linked together, spread and impact happens. The PLV—performance, learning-adaptation, and vitality—of those parts working at scale will create impact.

From those simple three parts, biology self-organizes epidemics from nothing to something. By infinitely improvising the types of pathogen, infection, and contagion, epidemics display the emergence we expect to see in complex adaptive systems, a whole greater than the sum of its parts. The process of viral resistance to the vaccine is an example. How does the virus "know" how to beat the vaccine? In essence, this "knowledge" emerges as an effective counter to the vaccine by the random sifting of thousands of innumerable mutations against the "laboratory" of host immune systems. The odds of success go up as the number of pathogen-host combinations—disease cases—in the human population increase. Once a disease is sufficiently widespread, multiple successes off this prototyping are inevitable. It's just how the math of biology works. If the exponential advantage for leaders in complex scenarios is PLV at scale, embedded and stabilized in human networks where continued sustained adaptation and spread is possible, the amazing miracle of epidemics is how they do it by the almost unfathomable process of self-organization, which creates new order and new possibilities simultaneously.

From Simple Parts to Organizing Principles

Self-organization itself is the magic sauce of any epidemic. You can potentiate it, observe it, harvest it, but you can't control it or make it happen any more than you can make people fall in love or commit themselves to a worthy cause. But it happens—often! In fact, it happens so regularly that a secondary wonder is how often leaders ignore it or fail to take advantage of it. Self-organization is truly mind boggling, even more so because it's neither random nor occasional. Like all the limitless "both-and" combinations floating around in a complex world, you do not have to abandon "directed organization" to tap the power of self-organization. They can work together.

I heard as concise an explanation I have ever heard of the underlying elements of self-organization at the Mayo Conference on Complexity in Health Care at the Mayo Clinic in April of 2004. My quest to understand exponential phenomena had taken me there after a colleague had scrawled Dee Hock's defining complexity quote on my whiteboard at work:

> *Simple clear purpose and principles give rise to complex, intelligent behavior. Complex rules and regulations give rise to simple, stupid behavior.*

(It's worth repeating, again and again.)

I was not sure what to expect at a conference on complexity and health care. What I found was a flea market mixture of innovators, neuroscientists, doctors, systems designers, and, to use their term, positive deviants. They had gathered to share research and approaches to knotty, entangled problems, the kind that you make worse if you approach them without checking your own assumptions and approaches early and often. There were stories, there were papers, there were mathematical models, there were conversations. Their problems were as varied as their backgrounds: how to increase health care quality without creating rigid delivery that didn't adapt to patient variation; how to increase patient participation and success in health when the encounter with formal health care was just tiny percentages of the time and attention when health accumulated or eroded; how to design simplicity in bureaucracies; how to comprehend population vitality as stability and instability; how the brain can create a subjective reality by responding to an objective one and vice versa.

As I sat in the auditoriums of one of the most reputable health care organizations in the world, new language framed my medical and leadership challenge: *How do we respond effectively in chaotic environments when things need to happen and you can't make them happen fast enough?* This dilemma hits home for emergency physicians early and hard. No matter how much we plan, the combination and timing of illness and injury always blows up our plan. The same challenge had hung in the air across my career everywhere from the trauma bay to the boardroom and beyond.

I found myself sitting in a workshop led by a woman named Glenda Eoyang. She now heads the Human Systems Dynamics Institute (`HSDInstitute.org`). She had spent years probing complexity via her background in mathematics and physics. I remember thinking I had finally stumbled on a framework that explained how biology was so unbelievably consistent, exponentially adaptable, and infinitely varying. She went over a lot of things that day, but her framework for how things self-organize has stuck with me since. Three things have to be in place for self-organization to occur, she said. If those things are in place, you can't be sure exactly what will happen, but some kind of pattern will emerge. The three things are a "container" where things can come together, a "defined interaction" that determines how objects will collide, and a "multiplier" of collisions. To launch epidemic action in your leadership work, leaders can link pathogen-infection-contagion by these principles as well.

Epidemics Require "Originating Conditions"

For things to self-organize, they require some kind of container or "field." The simple example of a soccer game illustrates this principle. If the "pathogen" is soccer, and the infection is the uptake of soccer concepts into playing skills and motivation (the "disease") in enough people to cause a soccer game, and if a "soccer culture" is the contagious spread of "soccer disease" among a population, there can't *be* any soccer unless there's a field somewhere, a container where "soccer" can happen, where soccer players can gather. The fields can be somewhat variable—dirt fields, turf fields, fields with lights, fields with goals that have nets versus those that don't, but without a field of some sort, you can't have a soccer game, and you can't have an epidemic of soccer. People can drift in and out of the field for work, dinner, sleep, and family, but when they enter the field, the field makes soccer possible and likely. The field says, "Here, soccer can happen."

Field effects influence all particles in a system, directly or indirectly. The sun, for example, exerts a field effect on the entire Earth, even though some of the Earth is in darkness when it's rotated away from the moon. Sunlight's effects on the environment are real, even if you personally never go outside in the sun. Put together the right combination of spaces and field effects, and you have a breeding ground for an epidemic. Put together the wrong spaces and effects, and your epidemic will never get going. Malaria requires field conditions that entail standing water in certain temperatures where certain species of mosquitoes can breed and multiply. You won't find malaria in a desert—too dry, too hot, too severe.

If you're going to lead a positive disease, it has to have somewhere to incubate and bubble. Knowing how to perceive, define, and create "originating conditions" becomes a key leadership skill.

Epidemics Require "Defined Interaction"

If you want things to self-organize within fields and containers, you've got to have "collisions" or "exchanges" or "reactions" among particles. By defining the nature of the interaction, the system has a defining element. Your "container" might be a glass of water. If you add salt to that water, we all know you get saltwater, not cranberry juice, every single time. Why? In saltwater, every collision of atoms in the water is between a positive sodium ion and a negative chloride ion. Assuming the water molecules form the "field" in the glass container in this chemical example, sodium and chloride in water depict two kinds of particles. Further, water influences both sodium and chlorine to form ions with a charge, but sodium becomes positive and chlorine becomes negative. Similarly, charged particles (Cl^- and Cl^- or Na^+ and Na^+) repel each other in water; opposite particles (Na^+ and Cl^-) attract each other. Those are the only two ways the particles can interact, the only two "interaction rules" possible in normal saltwater conditions. There are billions of atoms, but those are the rules that define collision and interaction.

In our soccer example, the field has to have certain particles—people and a ball. The particles known as people can interact with the ball or with other people—cooperatively as teammates and competitively as opposing players. The design of those interactions defines the game. In soccer, players have to use their feet. They are not blindfolded. One group tries to move the ball one direction by passing foot to foot; one group tries to move the ball the other, but they still have to interact by passing foot to foot (or rather, without using their arms and hands). If you had different "interaction rules"—players passing hand to hand to another team across a net, you'd have volleyball, even if you had the same people or "particles." Within fields and containers, the "rules of interaction" define how things bump into each other.

In an epidemic, there are two kinds of interaction rules—those that define how the pathogen interacts with the host it lands in, and those that define how two people with the disease interact with those who don't yet have it. Influenza, for example, first interacts with you by attaching to the lining of your mouth, nose, and airways. From there, it follows an amazing and annoying set of interactions within your body that result in the fevers, headaches, chills, body aches, burning cough, and throbbing eyeballs that add up to "I can't even get out of bed." *Infection*, the process by which a pathogen moves from a "possible disease" to "multiplying within the host," follows preset interaction rules between the virus and your cells.

For an epidemic to happen, as we know, we need contagion also—the spread from person to person. Once influenza has captivated your system, it goes about making millions of copies of itself, which flood through the channels and spaces of your bodies and invade still more of you. At least some of those particles have to leap *outside* your body to another person in order for a new infection and thus a new case of disease to erupt. How does that happen? Well, with influenza, it can happen via handshake, coughing, sharing water glasses, and so forth—influenza has a lot of simple "interaction rules" that support *contagion*, the transfer of pathogen between people. That's why it spreads so easily. On the other hand, human papilloma virus, or HPV, which causes cervical cancer in women, has to be spread by sexual contact. Shaking hands, hugging, sneezing, and snapchatting cannot spread that pathogen from one person to another.

How does interaction relate to leadership? As a leader, you can interact a certain way and have an impact in your interactions. You can show curiosity and shift how a one-on-one conversation goes or how a team responds to you. You can focus on results or choose to interact in a way that invites free spirited exploration. All of those create some sort of effect within and from and around you. If you are thinking of leadership as scaling PLV, you either have to get in every single interaction yourself, or you have to think about creating repeating rippling patterns of interaction. Change interaction, and you can shift whether you are playing soccer or volleyball. Define the nature of interaction and you can shift the effects which show up as PLV.

Epidemics Require Multipliers

In essence, in order to create any sort of sizeable impact, any potent interaction occurring in a field has to repeat over and over. Even things we think are very big, like gigantic rocks, are repetitions of smaller molecular arrangements. The Sun, for example, is a powerful nuclear source of energy not because of its one nuclear fusion reaction, which produces heat and light (which is powerful in itself), but because it has billions and billions of them. Your body is a coherent person not because *10* cells follow certain rules for taking in oxygen and expelling carbon dioxide, but because *300 hundred trillion cells*, whatever their function (eyeball or lung), are multiplying the effect of any particular oxygen metabolization "interaction rule" times 300 trillion.

Epidemics multiply by having more collisions with the host (10 people cough on you vs. 1, or 1 person coughs on you incessantly), more collisions within the host (100 viruses get in you vs. 1), and more potent, self-multiplying collisions—once the pathogen gets inside you, it doesn't just jump into one cell, it jumps into one cell, multiplies itself a thousand times, and reissues thousands of copies of itself back into your bloodstream to enter into numerous other cells and multiply again. You can have a great pathogen, a wonderfully nasty disease, and a widely connected network, but if you can't multiply the right kind of interactions, it's hard to get the disease going in one person, and it's hard to create the contagion that spreads it to others again and again.

Epidemics Move Through Networks, a Particularly Powerful Multiplier

In a system, things organize around nodes—places where things gather. In our soccer example, a player from whom and through whom a lot of passing happens would be a node. In our saltwater beaker example, you could put a negative electrode in the water, and it would attract positive ions—sodium. You could put a positive electrode in the water, and it would attract negative ions—chloride. Within the beaker, each of these charged electrodes is a node. You are a node, in a very literal sense. Certain things traffic to and from you: your co-workers' ideas, plans, and tasks; your family's daily calendar, dinner plans, ideas for vacation, social media posts. You are linked together with other nodes, called people, in a certain pattern. That pattern of nodes and connections is a network, and it's every bit as much a network as a computer network or a wireless network or a terrorist network. The ideas, actions, and function of the network may be very different, but in a foundational way, networks share fundamental design and function patterns. Biology traffics in networks—networks are how life moves genes, diseases, habits.

In our soccer example, some of the players from our field know other players *not* on that field who play on other fields, and sometimes players who know each other end up playing together on different fields. Diseases spread through networks as well. Intuitively, we all know this—if you're sick with the flu, you're most likely to get it from the people you bump into most—people in your family, at work, at your health club, at school. You may get it from someone at the grocery store, but if you add up all the other "nodes" who you bump into, you realize the number of possible "contagion touchpoints" is far higher from people you bump into most often (the network) who you interact with a certain way (hugs, coughs, handshakes). Assuming you have an equal chance of getting infected via contagion from any of these given contacts (which is usually not true in the real world), your probability is highest from your nearby, frequent contacts. Curiously, network spread behaviorally doesn't always follow the same patterns, depending on whether a behavior is "simple" or "complex," as we will see in Chapter 9.

Self-organization is the path epidemics take from their ineffectual early simplicity to their impressive widespread effects, and it is a path leaders who seek capacity must understand if you intend to surf complexity rather than drown in it. You can sit around and wait for self-organizing to happen, and it will. You can watch epidemics pop up, and you can be sure epidemic action is at work where you are leading without your knowing it (see rumor networks, for example). You can also be intentional about it. You *cannot control self-organization* (or it wouldn't be self-organization), but you can facilitate it and harvest its effects, which cannot be completely known until they emerge, surprise-like, in that greater-than-sum way complexity unfolds. Self-organization in nonhuman systems is really about the interplay of complexity principles and network principles. In human environments, we get to add a third discipline—neuroscience, which helps us understand what makes the human brain do *x* or *y* (although we are a long way from truly understanding how the brain does things). Apropos of the complexity of the brain itself, the principles unfold in unpredictable and myriad ways, but they still hold.

Interestingly, some epidemics self-organize across the patterns of interaction in a system—the combinations of people bumping into people—cause a brief blip, and then recede, leaving the network of people they've touched unchanged. Influenza is transient in this way as a social phenomenon. It tends to make people miserable, even kills a small number, but the change it creates in the population is essentially transient. After the flu leaves you, you go back to normal. Other epidemics move across the networks of our population and leave a stable change behind. They shift things permanently. Human papilloma virus is one such pathogen. When you get it, the infection doesn't really cause any symptoms. You don't feel like you have a disease. Meanwhile, the virus inserts itself in your DNA, and it waits. Years later, if you are a female and you have a cervix, the disease can trigger changes in your cervical tissue that unleash cervical cancer.

Self-organizing fundamental simplicity into increasingly large effects, temporary or permanent, is perhaps the unexplored territory of leadership in this age of movements, collective intelligence, social networks, internet platforms, and VUCA in general. Biology, again, makes it wonderfully concrete beyond the conceptual mystery. Each person reading these words was formed from the donation of a randomized 50 percent of parental DNA from two different people. Put differently, your biological mother and father had a meeting, and their 50 percent DNA donations turned into 100 percent of your DNA where you began as a single cell in your mother's uterus (or less likely in a laboratory). Without a policy manual, a boss, or a company protocol, over the next 40 weeks you followed some simple rules—cell division, streaming, differentiation, and connection-making—and emerged into the world as a 300 trillion cell infant human. This we've-all-done-it journey is both miraculous and so commonplace that we barely stop to think about it. It's also remarkably replicable—it always results (in our case) in a human, not a hippo or a hamster, *and* we are always different and unique.

Epidemics are similarly replicable, at least at the level of pattern. Leaders can create wider systemic effects via "intentional self-organization." First, define a pathogen. Second, create supportive conditions. Third, define the essential interactions necessary for infection and contagion. Fourth, leverage multipliers.

All three of the epidemic stories I have mentioned so far have followed these patterns. All three were intentional and based on the principles of epidemics and the widespread participation and volition of the people in them. Self-organization is amazing and even mind boggling, and each of us already a product of it. As a leadership approach, it verges on secret weapon territory when you combine its power with your intentionality and good will. Understanding these organizing principles gives you, a single leader or a group of leaders, an approach to creating success in the chaos you're encountering and allows you to "beat the math" of all those things going on out there beyond your control.

The Mango Tree, a Year Later

I returned to HELP school a year later. Where there had been a dusty school yard filled with trash was now a neat and orderly set of paths between fruit and vegetable plots anchored with mango and avocado trees. I could not find a single piece of litter. Students had taken ownership for particular shrubs and trees in pairs. The soccer team, without shoes, had taken second place in the district. A music program flourished under a new teacher and had won first place in a local competition between schools. Young entrepreneurs flocked around a computer learning lab, and government officials visited the hydroponics fish-and-vegetable laboratory on the campus. Not all those things began anew after my two days with the teachers and the students, but everything had clearly exploded in growth and connection. As much as I was comfortable with positive epidemics, I was overwhelmed with inspiration and admiration. The people of HELP school had created an epidemic of good. After reflecting on what was missing in "humble and obedient," they had found an infectious and contagious new word, and that word would make all the difference.

II Creating Epidemics

5 The Potential Power of Pathogen

Some pathogens blossom into epidemics; some do not. To optimize the chances of going epidemic, the ideal pathogen is one that thrives in those originating conditions, has an easy mode of interaction with and transmission between hosts, and can multiply well despite resistance against it. Shaping an idea into an infectious pathogen and releasing it so that it is easily picked up, easily multiplied, and easily passed by epidemic action is a key leadership action. *Where* the idea comes from is not particularly important. It could come from you, someone in your team, a customer, or an already existing notion in your environment. What is essential is *how* the idea has the potential to move and result in positive effects in your system once you design self-organizing.

An Idea Core with Attracting Hooks

When Michael Bervell launched the epidemic known as Growth Groups at Microsoft in late 2019, his welcome email coupled two key needs of early-in-career (EIC) professionals at Microsoft: "to develop professionally alongside and create friendships with other EIC hires." Having been an undergraduate intern previously at Microsoft, he knew a thing or two about what EIC hires needed and lacked, and he had experience with a positive group social-mentoring experience in college. His knowledge of the emotional environment of his fellow EIC "hosts" shaped how he framed the idea. In essence, he was using selected words to create a hook, or an antigen, to pair with emotional "receptors" in potential participants—"patient zeros," as he would later call them. In his invitation, he built further hooks by linking company-wide conditions to further "antigens" on the surface of his idea, which he described to me as, simply, "to have a best friend at work":

> *Each "Growth Group" is an intentional, in-person microcosm of Microsoft's growth mindset culture and revolves around five themes:*
>
> 1. **1 percent better:** Becoming 1 percent better every day (based on Kaizen, a Japanese philosophy)
> 2. **Communication:** Discover and share the stories around you (based on David Isay's philosophy)
> 3. **Giving:** Contribute value to other "Growth Group" members (based on *Give and Take* by Adam Grant)
> 4. **Grit:** Get comfortable being uncomfortable (based on *Grit* by Angela Duckworth)
> 5. **Vulnerability:** Realize that people are people (based on *Dare to Lead* by Brené Brown)[1]

Like a good salesperson aware of the features and benefits that would appeal to a group of people looking for helpful context, he appealed to what he understood they would be seeking. Knowing there was a jarring bit of disorientation as they entered the cold realities of the corporate world after the nurturing security of college, he waved the prospect of helpful knowledge from people who had succeeded ahead of them:

> *Special guests (such as Microsoft EVPs, CVPs, and SVPs) will share their stories or professionals from outside of Microsoft will teach leadership curriculum (such as improv classes, public speaking, executive presence, and more).*[2]

Michael Bervell's initial introduction illustrates a central principle about the idea of creating a "social pathogen" as an act of leadership. Biological pathogens have some sort of genetic core that establishes their identity, either the DNA of bacteria and protozoan pathogens or DNA or RNA for viruses. Although this genetic material has all the code needed to build out every component in the entire pathogen—the DNA and RNA itself, cellular components for bacteria and protozoan, the viral "coating," called an envelope—it needs a way to attach to host cells. It attaches to receptors on host cells by linking to them with the hooks, or antigens, described in Chapter 3. If the genetic core is the blueprint for all the effects the pathogen will cause when infection allows it to create disease effects in a host, antigens are what allow that core to "stick" to the host so that infection can begin.

Within a short email, Michael Bervell had flashed just such an effective pathogen, a core idea wrapped in hooks that were "sticky" to his audience. You may not always get to pick the idea you are responsible for turning into action, but you can always modify it and "decorate" it with antigens uniquely targeted at the hosts you want to infect. In this case, Michael Bervell did get to pick his pathogen; he started an idea that was not yet there. He did not get to define Microsoft's emphasis on growth mindset (although he agreed with it), the sense of "social starvation," as one early Growth Group participant put it, which early-in-career tech hires can feel, or its need to create meaningful attraction for the young people it hired, but he effectively used these ideas to create antigen-hooks on his core idea. He did get to mesh the promise of helpful corporate context and mentoring guidance from senior executives for a not-yet-committed workforce with an unspoken but powerful need in Microsoft's early-in-career population. "Find a best friend at work."

He wasn't sure how it would work. He was just hoping to get a couple of groups bubbling to help him create a positive peer experience at Microsoft. Was he trying to solve a corporate engagement challenge in a company that one Growth Group member described as "not exactly loved by the kids"? Was he trying to solve the existential career crisis for the talented young people who had landed a coveted first tech job? Not really. Bervell himself is mild-mannered, insatiably curious, and emphatic about social innovation. Having been at Microsoft as an intern, he viewed his job there as a convenient opportunity in his native Seattle area, but he wasn't star struck. "When I was hired, I assumed I wouldn't be at Microsoft very long," he told me. He was aware of the company's need to hold young talent, and he personally resonated with his fellow EICs' personal-professional predicament of needing to find a niche in a vast company. Given his own professional goals, his motivation was singular even as he designed it with others' well-being in mind. "I wanted to hyperscale my network," he shrugged. "I knew there were future colleagues and connections out there, so I just decided to create a new network and see what came out of it. I would need it for whatever came next." Intentional, unpredictable.

The world is filled with biological pathogens, and it is filled with ideas that *could* travel and multiply but don't. Of the countless pathogens—would-be diseases and epidemics—hanging around, most of them are locked up in stable systems. Your gut, for example, is home to as many bacteria, roughly, as the number of cells in your entire body.[3] Your team, company, and neighborhood certainly harbor a lot of contained ideas not yet on the move. Once released to flow freely from their stable location in an ecosystem, pathogens don't all cause the same degree of effect. Many don't bloom into epidemics. The ones that create powerful effects are most impressive at expressing disease. Epidemiologists refer to this property in a pathogen as "virulence," or the "relative capacity of a pathogen (such as a bacterium or virus) to overcome a host's defenses and cause disease or damage."[4] Part of the virulence comes from the impact contained in the genetic map, the code that can multiply into disease within a host. Another aspect of virulence comes from the antigenic array on the surface of pathogens, which can make it easier or more difficult for that genetic core, or your core idea, to "get inside" the people you lead. As you think about the epidemic you'd like to call up, it is critical to define your intended pathogen very intentionally in its core concept and its "hooks." Your epidemic will grow and create impact easier if you can shape a basic idea into positive virulence.

Whether you dream it up yourself, coalesce if from a collaborative collegial effort, or support an established corporate norm, your pathogen will need to support its own self-organizing growth through the infection and contagion in your group of people, against the resistance and "immunity" in any human social system. Your ability to design an idea that intrinsically optimizes the odds of that self-organizing process is essential. It will have to coexist, hopefully positively, with that more formal organizational operating system of org charts, policies, protocols, and norms. The degree to which you can design a pathogen that is particularly infectious, resistant to your organizational immune system, and virulent will go a long way toward determining how well it can self-organize and sustain an epidemic.

In their book *Made to Stick*, Chip and Dan Heath talk about the attributes which make an idea "sticky." In essence, they're talking about social virulence. They use the acronymic model of SUCCESS. In their model of an effective idea, S stands for simple, U for unexpected, C for concrete, the second C for credible, E for emotional, and S for stories. The last S remains a grab bag for the idea maker, and it handily rounds out the acronym.[5]

Against the Heaths' model for an effective idea, Michael Bervell's "best friend at work" idea stands up pretty well. He wrapped the antigens of professional development, exposure to senior execs from inside and outside the company who had found success on their own journeys, and the four-point dimensions of growth mindset (Bervell's framing, not Microsoft's) around a *simple* core idea. It was certainly *unexpected*; people randomly got an email from a guy they hadn't heard of with a potential answer to a personal professional itch. His invitation was *concrete* with details, dates, and a clear call to action:

> *Joining a "Growth Group" is a 5-month, one-hour-per-week commitment from November 1, 2019 to March 31, 2020. Unfortunately only EICs in Redmond or Bellevue can participate this season. Even if you do not end up joining, I recommend checking out the links above.*
>
> *Questions? Email us!*
>
> *Thanks —hopefully, you find this interesting!*[6]

He was a *credible*, early-in-career person himself. Although not overly emotional, his invitation reached a widely felt *emotional* need in his colleagues that he recognized. As for the S, he specifically invites his colleagues to "discover and share the stories."

The SAND Pneumonic

Your epidemic-starting idea, whatever it is, will need to thrive in all the complexity inherent in modern circumstances. As we recognize, epidemics have wild and unpredictable turns and dimensions you can't control. For that reason, and building on the Heath brothers' idea of simplicity, I like the pneumonic acronym SAND. It helps me remember that the small grains add up to the uncountable beach. The SAND pneumonic for pathogen design is as follows:

S = Simple

For all the reasons that simplicity works in both complex environments and on the preoccupied human brain, the simple idea *works*. If your core idea can't be grounded in simple terms, it's not going to move very well or very fast, no matter how brilliant or helpful it is. As Einstein said, "Any darn fool can make something complex; it takes a genius to make something simple." Just saying you want it to be simple doesn't make it so. We sometimes hear about the need to "dumb it down," an unfortunate phrase that is the antithesis of the clarity and possibility you will want an epidemic to evoke. As Einstein also said, "Everything should be made as simple as possible, but no simpler." It can take time, and quite a bit of listening, to crystallize apparently different ideas and perspectives floating around you into a simple, foundational idea. Think of this simple idea as the core of your pathogen. It's the genetic material that will multiply in your system via an epidemic. It still needs antigens so people can latch onto it, become infected, become diseased, and become contagious.

A = Attractive Antigens

By attractive, we don't mean romantically alluring but, rather, personally compelling. In the complexity literature, the concepts of "attractors" and "repellers" denote conditional elements that bring objects closer or push them farther away. A magnetic field is an attractor for iron filings, but not an attractor for wood. Wind blowing from you toward a pile of sawdust is a repeller for the tiny wood particles (relative to your location). The universe is filled with infinite attractors and repellers, with different combinations for different particles and substances, acting in all different directions. Fish are attracted to water, for instance, whereas polar bears are repelled by heat.

The people who will create the epidemic from the ideas you are framing are, no doubt, similar in some ways and different in others. Understanding what is universally attractive and repellent to them requires careful listening to their mindsets, perspectives, and experiences to help you frame the thought pathogen that you might want to release into an epidemic where you work. Michael Bervell understood that professional development, contact with others who had been successful and might have career "cheat codes," and a chance to create connection with other early-in-career employees were attractors. He also understood that both social isolation and the disorientation of being young and new in a company where thousands of people were already established were repellers. He put the attractors in front of people and the repellers behind them as he framed his Growth Groups pathogen.

"Attraction" always has to be framed with the host audience in mind. Later in the epidemic, when those host-people have become contagious, they will also need to think about keeping the thought-pathogen attractive for others. First, though, it's your job. These "attractors" can change just as viruses and bacteria can change their antigens to become more infectious, as we saw SARS-Cov-2 do throughout the Covid-19 pandemic.

The author Daniel Pink does a nice job of articulating what is universally attracting to people in his book *Drive*, which frames the central principles that motivate people intrinsically. Pink reveals how a lot of things that we *think* motivate people, particularly the way we perceive external incentives, actually don't (and unfortunately are widely codified in business practices and accepted myths about motivation). He reviews how the concepts of mastery, the chance to be good at something; autonomy, the chance to make free decisions and be free of compulsory compliance; and purpose, the reason that we do something, are all powerful intrinsic motivators. They are just waiting for the right pathogen-antigen combinations to attract us.

Pink's work refers to earlier research by researchers Richard Ryan and Edward Deci, the founders of Self-Determination Theory. The cornerstones of intrinsic motivation according to their research are the three basic human needs for *competence* (mastery per Pink), *autonomy*, and *relatedness* (purpose for Pink). Relatedness is significant because self-organization—the growth of your epidemic—is grounded in how objects relate in a system. Crafting your pathogen—both its simple core idea and its supportive antigens—around how the people who will host and spread the idea becomes critical. Create a pathogen that invites the opportunity to be good at something, the ability to decide freely, and the chance to connect to work, self, and colleagues, and your core idea will be more attractive. As we will see when we explore the multiplying effect of networks, how we relate and with whom we relate are powerful influencers of how we think, act, and interact.

N = Novel

The human brain has the same paired tendencies we can see throughout complex adaptive systems, and one of these pairings is *novel-normal* or *unique-usual*. Throw the brain too much novel and unique and it will long for normal and usual; throw it too much normal and usual and it will seek novel, the "shiny object." One reason we like vacations and weekends is that they are a break from the endless, rote routine of weekdays. Of course, if "novel and unique" become too out of the norm, they create fear and anxiety, which is a poor state for taking in new ideas. Much of our work is filled with a lot of "do the same thing, day after day." For that reason, even as you seek to introduce a pathogen that will eventually help define a new normal steady state, creating a sense of curiosity, a promise of the invitingly different, is key. No one expected Michael Bervell to come up with a grassroots, out-of-nowhere, new idea. It wasn't even categorizable against the daily norm of life at Microsoft for new hires. The curious brain is more receptive than the criticizing brain; the inquiry is a more potent receptive state than inquisition. If you're hoping to create an epidemic of PLV, the way you frame your thought pathogen, your change-making idea, must induce curiosity and inquiry. You cannot do this alone, merely by describing an idea, but you can create a really good start.

D = Dual Interest

Your pathogen is going to have to multiply across the biodiversity of an entire population. Whether that group is a team, a group of teams, an eclectic group of different disciplines, or a whole company, that population comprises a wide variety of individual nuances of motivation and preference. Your idea has to be amenable and applicable to that personal palette of mastery-competence, autonomy-volition, and purpose-relatedness. The axiom WIIFM, *what's in it for me,* refers to this reality. We often hear, on occasions when someone puts themselves above or beyond the needs of a team or community, "don't put yourself above the team," or "it's not about you." These are nice things to say, but it's also true that every living thing seeks its own PLV, its own well-being. It is biologically encoded.

That encoded self-interest does not necessarily make people anti-altruistic or poor team players (though many self-interested people clearly do not behave altruistically). That self-interest, in the midst of a larger collective interest—team, business unit, company, community, institution—does mean that if your thought pathogen is going to encounter minimal resistance and compel optimal attraction, it had better appeal to both the micro elements of self-interest and the more macro element of collective interest. Imagine if Michael Bervell's email had contained antigens that repelled senior leaders at Microsoft. "Learn how to take down everything Microsoft has done!" The response from senior leaders to his efforts may well have been not yes, no, or ignore. The response may have been, "This is not happening." Epidemics are fragile at first, and pathogens have to get past immune systems before they have the adaptive and scale advantages they will later accrue.

Rousing intrapersonal or organizational resistance simply makes it harder for the idea core of your pathogen to travel. Any pathogen will encounter some individuals who are somewhat immune, but it's a leadership error to neglect population-based resistance to an idea that you want to be accepted at the individual and group level. The best pathogens shouldn't just create attraction at the self or group level. The best pathogens should set the stage for a greater awareness that self and group are mutually beneficial—that "I" and we" are linked together positively. Creating antagonism or an either-or choice along that front will likely doom your epidemic or create an epidemic that launches a divisive social war across loci of authority and status. Bets are off at that point. This focus on avoiding early resistance is not about acquiescing to false values or compromised ethics; it is about creating momentum early with a new idea. Companies are often loaded with this sort of tension, which they often try to address ad hoc with "engagement initiatives." Don't embed that risk early in your pathogen design.

Naming the HELP Pathogen

After our initial afternoon conversation in Masese at HELP school, the teachers went home in the evening after our conversation about "something from nothing" to think about what new words they might want in the children's heads. Before we gathered again under the old mango tree the following day, I had a chance to listen to the seventh-grade class, the oldest class in the school.

They were accustomed to giving "right answers," and I really wanted their unvarnished thoughts. I had them pair up and ask each other to name their dreams. As we got back together after a few minutes, I asked them to name their dreams out loud. Silence, of course, at first. Then there were a few cautious hands. Like kids the world over, their dreams ran from the typical to the novel to the surprising. Several wanted to be pastors, doctors, and teachers. One wanted to be a pilot. One wanted to be an HR executive. I would not have predicted that one. When I was in seventh grade, I didn't even know what HR was. I would have said it stood for "home run."

"What did it feel like to name your dream?" I asked. "What was it like to speak it out loud."

Silence.

"Do you often speak your dreams out loud?"

"No," they all said.

"So what did it feel like?"

"It was fun," one little girl said. "And scary."

"How so?" I asked the girl who had spoken up.

"When I say my dream, it feels like it will really happen, but it is scary because I don't know if people will laugh at me."

Another student added on, "And I don't know how to make my dream come true!"

"Who talks to you about your dream?" I asked them. I had them break into pairs again, different combinations. When they were done, they had a list: parents, friends, pastors, teachers.

A young boy held his brow furrowed while he listened to the flurry of responses. At least half of the class had a similar expression on their faces.

"You look like you have a thought," I said to him. "What are you thinking?"

"No one talks to me about my dream," he said. The quiet half of the classroom nodded.

"Do you think your teachers can help you with your dream?" I asked them.

"Yes!" they all said together.

"I want you to help me understand how the teachers can help you. Think about not what they explain about their subject, but about how they can help you grow your dream." They broke into separate pairs again. The room escalated into noise and laughter as they talked.

"Well, what did you come up with? What ideas do you have?"

"We would like them to show us how they made their dream come true." "We would like to know if they changed their dream or if they stuck to one dream." "I want to know what they did when they didn't think they could make it." "How did they find the way?"

"Okay, thank you!" I said. "I will be talking with the teachers after school. May I have your permission to share your thoughts with them?"

"Yes!"

After school, as the children lingered in loose groups across the brick-fenced school yard, kicking soccer balls and playing tag, the teachers and staff and I gathered again in the circle in the shade.

"What thoughts did you have?"

"I thought about God," said one teacher. "When God started, there was nothing. When God was done, there was everything. I asked myself what God did. God CREATED the world, and we are in God's image. So I think the word we need is 'creativity,' but it must not be only a word. It has to be how we think, all the time. We must ask ourselves, 'What is creativity, right now, everywhere?'"

My thought going in was that we would have some meandering discussion, but there were so many nods along with his remarks. "We want to add 'creativity' to 'humble' and 'obedient,'" they said. "We will start tomorrow."

At the next day's assembly, with the children's classes lined in parallel columns facing the teachers who were going over the day's announcements, they introduced the new word.

"Children," one young teacher said from the front of the lines, "we will be adding a new word to everything we do. Do you understand?" Her voice was strong and found every small set of eyes.

"Yessssss!" they all chanted in unison.

"When I say, 'How are you?' you say what to me?"

"We are humble and obedient!"

"Now we want you to say, 'We are humble and obedient and *creative*!' Are you ready?"

"Yesssss!"

"Students, how are you this morning?!"

"We are humble and obedient and *creative*!"

They had found their new word.

That day in the dust, the teachers had a core idea, and it would take some time to shape it into a pathogen that went epidemic, but it began that day with a question and an answer. Creativity would be their pathogen.

Notes

1. Michael Bervell, email communication to author, January 30, 2021.
2. Ibid.

3. Ron Sender et al., "Revised Estimates for the Number of Human and Bacteria Cells in the Body," *PLoS Biology* 14, no. 8 (August 19, 2016): https://dx.doi.org/10.1371%2Fjournal.pbio.1002533.
4. "Virulence," Merriam-Webster.com Dictionary, accessed December 20, 2020, https://www.merriam-webster.com/dictionary/virulence?src=search-dict-box.
5. "Made to Stick Success Model," www.MADEtoSTICK.com, 2008, https://heathbrothers.com/download/mts-made-to-stick-model.pdf.
6. Michael Bervell, email communication to author, January 30, 2021.

6 Creating Conditions

> *Other seeds fell into the good soil, and as they grew up and increased, they yielded a crop and produced thirty, sixty, and a hundred times as much.*
>
> —*Mark 4:8*

Like all self-organizing phenomena, epidemics require originating conditions. You could have the perfect pathogen and a very susceptible host, but if conditions don't enhance the chance of productive collisions between pathogen and hosts and again among hosts, infection and contagion can't happen. Without the right conditions, your epidemic will never get going.

SARS-CoV-2 has some handy features as a pathogen—it can linger suspended in the air for a while, and its antigens lock easily into some key receptors in our bodies—but without a supportive environment, it cannot move explosively in the currents of our populations. Fortunately for the virus and unfortunately for us, the virus found its supportive conditions. The human body itself is a convenient and accessible container, loaded with docking receptors and capable of multiplying the virus by the millions. Crowding is a condition that works—stadiums, bars, parties, large get-togethers all potentiate contagion. Ventilation is another; places that are enclosed allow transmission better than open, windy areas. Even our social hesitation is a condition; as we wondered how to deal with it and devolved from rapid experimentation and transfer of knowledge to political narrative battles, it exploited our divisions and uncertainty and kept us from acting as one to eliminate it.

Your leadership epidemic needs generative conditions, too. Without them, the patterns that support performance, learning, and vitality can't get going, can't grow, and can't sustain. You can—and will—have all sorts of ideas and talent lying dormant within the people around you and never see them blossom into an infectious trend in your team or organization. For leaders seeking to create truly systemic effects, whether in small team environments or across larger populations, shaping conditions is foundational to your epidemic.

Spaces, Containers, and Fields

Supportive conditions can be spaces, containers, or fields. Spaces can be physical locations like rooms or stadiums or parks. Containers can be procedural containers like meetings or routines where people predictably gather or interact. Think of fields as shared "experience clouds" or context that people can move in and through, but perhaps not permanently. Magnetic fields are great examples of physical fields; wind is another. A collective emotional experience is a kind of field; when people participate in the experience together, it has a certain effect, even though that effect is slightly different in each person and they may not even be in the same place when they experience it. Fields can be physiological states that potentiate receptivity, insight, awareness, and intentionality. Fields can be mental states that shape how we respond to ideas and concepts.

There are infinite contextual elements in any environment, of course. Right now you are reading these words in an environment whose conditions feature air, which further contains oxygen, nitrogen, and carbon dioxide. The air is a certain temperature. You may be inside or outside. You are subject to gravity, which exerts another field effect. Some of the conditions around you and within you create effects that are relevant to your immediate awareness, like that cold wind blowing through the open door. Others are less relevant to your immediate concerns, like the effect of lunar gravity on the planet's tides, or the insulin resistance that is leading you toward diabetes without your feeling it.

As you set the conditions—spaces, containers, and fields—for positive epidemic action, you do *not* need to set infinite conditions (and you couldn't, in any case), and you do not want to establish complicated conditions. You do want to consider which conditions optimally invite a positive interaction between your idea pathogen and the hosts, those people who will internalize and multiply that idea pathogen into epidemic effect. Prioritizing and emphasizing a few key conditions that create traction for your positive pathogen and increase receptivity in host participants is enough to get things going.

Conditions tend to affect everyone in the space, container, or field whether the space is small, like a meeting room or a single individual's brain, or large, like a full football stadium influenced by a flashing scoreboard saying "*Noise!*" Just as sunlight and soil affect every plant in a garden, these conditions affect everyone in that space. Setting them well—and sustaining them—vastly increases the odds of the infection and contagion that fuel the shift in patterns of thought, action, and interaction that will carry your epidemic. Some conditions will be specific to your particular performance–learning–vitality focus. The conditions that favor reliability and precision, for example, may be different from those that favor innovation and experimentation. You can set conditions as specifically as you need to for particular pathogens and populations.

Nonetheless, we do have sound scientific knowledge about more universal conditions that favor human uptake and transmission of new ideas. We understand increasingly what helps humans turn an idea into an action and action into a habit. We know that our brains are capable of changing their own internal patterns, a property called *neuroplasticity*. In essence, to create an epidemic, leaders will want to potentiate individual and group neuroplasticity so that individuals readily adopt and pass on new ideas, acting as both receivers and authors of new patterns of thought, action, and interaction. Think of these conditions as containers or fields that potentiate the infectious and contagious trafficking of the idea pathogen you are trying to spread.

A Man and a Horse

Over 20 years ago, I encountered the power of conditions when I watched a man work with a young horse. I found myself leaning on the edge of a round corral 30 feet across in the receding heat of a long summer day. Brandon Carpenter was a sturdy, energetic guy with a bushy moustache and thick hands from working with wire and rope. He wore the standard ranch uniform: wrangler jeans, boots with a riding heel, and a big belt buckle anchoring his button work shirt. I had followed his purposeful stride from the driveway of his place to the small round corral where a young horse stood in the dust.

The second he let himself in the pen, Brandon's demeanor changed. The man with almost projectile energy and intense gaze softened into quiet ease. His voice dropped, and his movements slowed. The horse had its eyes and ears on him before he even got in the pen, and I settled on the rail to watch.

For the next half hour, I watched the man and the horse work together. I had seen people and horses work together my whole life, and I had never seen anything like how Brandon worked a horse that evening. The animal moved in circles left and right, speeding up, slowing down, stopping and turning on nearly invisible cues. Brandon stood in the middle of the circle and moved very little, his body shifting slightly one way or the other, his voice encouraging but steady, his hands pointing one way or the other. I had very little idea of what he was doing, but the horse did. The animal was attentive, committed, and responsive. He was not under any physical control from Brandon at all—no ropes, no bridle, no gear at all. Brandon didn't say anything the first few minutes. Then he started to narrate.

"This horse is about two weeks in. We started working about 15 minutes at a time. Young horses are like young people. Their brains shut down after a bit until they get used to working. You can't really do anything with a horse until you create trust. For a horse, life is pretty simple. They either think they're safe, or they think they're not. At that point, fight-or-flight kicks in, and they're moving away in more or less of a hurry, depending on how bad the threat is. If they're cornered they'll fight."

"Makes sense," I said. "How do you create the trust?"

"Well, that's the trick of it. They tend to trust other horses because they all play by the same rule, so the only question left is whether that horse gets to tell them what to do or they get to do the telling. If they're not sure, they argue about it. If they have an easy time of it, very little happens. A couple ears go back, the other animal agrees, and they're done. If they both think they're the one to give the orders, things can get physical. They'll bite, rear up and strike each other, body check each other, swing their hips and mule kick until one of them backs down. Once they figure it out, that's the way it goes, and they're both good. Until one of them decides to bring up the issue again, which happens from time to time.

"The problem is, when they work with us, they need to trust us and respect us, but you can't safely get into a physical argument with a horse on your own. If you tie them down and hit them with things, they'll get the dominance piece from you, but now you've got a scared animal, which is a dangerous animal at some point, and trust is shot. Plus you're just showing you don't have the tools to lead very well, and they will never give you everything they could. Depending on how they've been treated, they may not be afraid of humans, but the trust you need to work with them on anything important has to be stronger than just passive tolerance. It has to be built and tested. You're going to ask them to do things they've never done and wouldn't on their own, repeatedly by the way, and they have to trust themselves and you both. You have to earn it, and so do they."

"It seems easier to build on once it's started," I said.

"Absolutely. And sometimes, just like anything else, you have bad days. And with a young horse, you can go backwards, and then you have to slow down and back it up a bit."

"So where do you start?"

"What do you mean? What do we ask a horse to do at first, or how do you I get them to trust me?"

"The trust part."

"Think of a horse as a mirror to whatever's going on in your body. Whichever way you are inside is going to affect how they are. Their brains may not be as big as ours, but they notice everything. *Everything*. They get nervous if they don't trust you, and they actually get stressed if they don't have this dominance thing figured out either, because their nerves are telling them to either assert themselves or trust that you can assert yourself to their advantage, which again, is safety. They can't trust you if you're not at ease; your hesitation triggers theirs. They don't like mixed signals. Step one is get yourself and the horse calm, and step two is get them listening to you. They actually kind of happen at the same time." He adjusted his straw cowboy hat and wiped the sweat from his forehead with his sleeve. "Here, I'll show you."

He turned back to the horse. "Let's move, boy. There you go . . . good, good." The horse broke into motion, easy and unrushed, its muscles lax and fluid. "Now, I'm going to get him to go faster in a second. I could do it by hand cues, by shifting my weight and distance with regard to the horse, or with my energy." To make sure I understood, he asked, "What's my energy like right now?"

"Pretty relaxed, I'd say."

"Exactly. And the horse is relaxed also. Hear how his feet land quiet in the dust, and see his head is alert but not up high? If you look close, you can see his muscles are loose. Now . . . watch this." He clicked once with his mouth, and the horse broke into a run. After the animal did a couple laps around the pen, Brandon said one word, his voice dropping into a slow sigh, "Easy . . ." The horse dropped out of a run and into a walk as if someone had pulled a power plug. "Good, good . . . boy . . . whoa . . ." the horse stopped on the last word, its eyes and ears on Brandon, waiting. It made a chewing motion.

"See that, that chewing?"

"Yeah."

"That's him saying, 'I get it. I'm listening.' I could have said and done the same things, but if my energy was different, the horse would have had a harder time responding, or he would have panicked into speed instead of committed into it. A lot of times we give a horse the wrong signal with our energy, thinking we've given them the right one with our technical cues."

"Doesn't that screw them up?"

"Well, yes, if you're not paying attention. But if they trust you, they basically tell you they're confused, and you notice, and you get clear. Happens all the time. In fact, getting confused with them is one way you and they get better. You're both always learning, but you have to be listening, and there has to be trust. You have to trust them also. They always pick the strongest signal from you if you're giving them conflicting cues. And they're always right."

We talked a few more minutes, and what stuck with me was how Brandon was often doing two things at once that seemed in tension. He was encouraging the horse to move with liberty and ease, and he was defining firm boundaries. He was working to be exquisitely clear in what he was telling the horse and how he wanted the horse to do it, but he was also listening intently to what the horse was telling him about how it was responding to him, what the horse was wanting, tolerating, resisting. Brandon was uncommonly positive, praising the horse for the slightest of efforts, but was demanding that those smallest things ultimately be done with precision. The results were certainly precise. At one point he had the horse move one step—one *foot*—and then stop again, several times in a row.

I did not think it was at all like watching paint dry. On the drive home, I kept seeing images of Genghis Khan's steppe warriors, mounted horsemen all, putting their horses into lying positions on the ground to ambush approaching armies from tall grass. I kept thinking of Native plains people, flitting in and out of running buffalo, killing their winter meat without their hands on their horses as they dodged the swinging heads of their prey at 35 miles per hour. I have been buying horses from Brandon ever since that day in the dust.

The Gravity of Conditions

A person and a horse pirouetting in a circle may seem a long way from a positive epidemic, but the horse-human dynamic in that dusty space was an example of a simple relational system, much like the ones that occur in limitless and overlapping combinations in organizations between colleagues, divisions, sellers, and buyers—and in epidemics. To this day, every time I step into the roundpen to work with my own horses or to help people encounter system principles by working with an unfettered horse, I think of the three kinds of conditions we need to be able to create intentional self-organization.

First Brandon demonstrated a mindset that I would not have been able to name at the time. He frequently referenced the idea of "always learning, every horse is different, you have to figure them all out one by one" and that no matter what you learned, whether it appeared to be a failure or a success, it was information for the next time. He saw these repeated encounters as necessary to his learning and certainly to the horse's. His own storehouse of knowledge from years of working with hundreds of horses was immense, but he was always learning more from each horse. Effort was more important than immediate success, and he lavished praise on the horse for the smallest of efforts and reassured the animal when it became confused. He also referred repeatedly to apparent opposites that were important for the horse to work well with him: to move freely, to respect boundaries; to project clearly, to understand attentively; to be firm, to be gentle; to project purposeful intention, to let the horse figure it out.

He also emphasized the point that none of his work could even happen if he and the horse were out in a 500-acre pasture. The horse might listen, but in all likelihood it would wander away and eat grass when it felt like it. Spatial structure was important to put the two of them in sufficient proximity where, without ropes and tack, they had to deal with each other. Something had to keep the two of them in the same space so they could work together without the binding effect of ropes and leather.

Finally (and I would learn more from him as he was willing to talk about it more over the ensuing years), he referred to what he called energy, and what in my medical language is physiology. Our nervous system is equipped with the same complementarity he embodied as he worked with the horse. It is equipped for flight-fight-freeze and for ease and unthreatened flow. It can snap into rote and automatic action, and it can entertain new ideas and uncertain realities. It can adhere to timeworn patterns or bend into new ones. None of it is accidental, and a particular brain state potentiates certain things and mitigates others. He and the horse were neurologically "wired together" while they worked. He built that mini neural network to create the effects he needed with the horse.

When we are in a threatened state, we really can't process new concepts. Our sympathetic nervous system turns on, and it focuses on immediate here-and-now imperatives that block out temporarily nonessential things like new ideas, creativity, deeper analysis, and new insights, all of which our brain can create and grasp only in a generative state. In VUCA settings, those situations that are volatile, uncertain, complex, ambiguous or any combination of those, the brain can function wonderfully *if* it is in the right mode. It can also buck and regress to automatic, this-is-what-I-do-quickly-always mode under stress, which doesn't work so well in VUCA environments. Interestingly, much of the time at work, or even in life, we are living against a backdrop of stress triggers. We rush along with crammed calendars, rapidly toggle from task to task, slog through long to-do lists, and simmer in relational tension with co-workers or "other" people that suboptimize our brains for VUCA function, not to mention for our own health.

The most fundamental conditions you have to set as a leader are really the ones Brandon had to set to optimize the work both he and the horse were doing. Social epidemics require mental conditions, the way people mentally frame events and circumstances. They also require spatial and structural conditions, the way people encounter each other physically. Finally, they require physiological conditions, the internal field that sets the brain for optimal intake, processing, and integration of new ideas and conversion of those ideas to insight and then to intent and action.

Just as there are infinite conditions—fields, spaces, and containers—in the universe, there are infinite conditions underlying our efforts at work, home, and public life. Some attract our better thoughts, actions, and interactions, and some are more repelling. Some you can create, and some you have accept. You can neither invent nor eliminate gravity, for example, but you can create and emphasize conditions that help people participate in epidemic action. Because what you are trying to get done varies, and so do the circumstances you are working in, you will continue to discover conditional elements that help your intended epidemic grow. There's an element of improvisation to shaping optimal conditions. You can start with a few and see what's working and what's not.

COVID did this, too. How could it have known ahead of time that political polarization or discordant communication between countries would be a condition that would help it move? Like Brandon, you have to keep "listening to the horse." Given what we have learned over the past couple of decades about human motivation, the neuroscience of behavior, and the power of social networks, though, a few key conditions emerge as having widely applicable value in creating human epidemics that are healthy and effective.

Thinking Conditions: Growth Mindset and Polarity Thinking

We know that adaptation and self-organization in complexity comprise endless iteration. We also know that complexity embodies the complementary pairs we mentioned in Chapter 3. Your leadership epidemic will have to flourish in similarly complex settings and will progress via relentless iteration and both-and facility on the part of participants. Because complex settings are embedded with countless tensions—order and chaos, individual ideas and collective alignment, for example—high-functioning teams need to be able to wield such complementary thinking themselves and together. It does not help them to lapse into black-white, either-or thinking in these circumstances. Further, we will only rarely get things right the first time. We have to keep trying, adjusting, trying again. Wherever you are leading, people will decide to what extent they will participate, whether to embrace the infection of a new idea, and whether to commit to being contagious in their own actions. The external environment around each of them will hold reasons why they should participate, but ultimately, they will get to decide.

For them to participate wholeheartedly, and consequently for your epidemic to really grow, those "host" people will need to be in the right frame of mind, equipped for the rough-and-tumble back and forth of new efforts and the tensions of opposing ideas. They'll have to do it in the setting of current and historical social pressure that often defines either-or thinking and short-term results as the dominant signals of our daily work lives. The individual and collective capacity for resilient iteration and both-and thinking will vastly serve epidemic action.

When Brandon ("Do not call me a whisperer!"), over 30 years into his work as a horse trainer told me, "I'm always learning, and so is anyone who works with a horse," he was voicing a mindset defined in 2006 by Carol Dweck in the book *Mindset*. The book articulates a framework for why some people continue to improve across their lives, sometimes reaching uncommon heights of accomplishment, while others, apparently equally talented at the beginning, regress to performance far less grand. She discovered in her research on intelligence that when people perceive the world, and themselves, as "fixed" in intelligence, they define themselves that way and live accordingly. When things don't go well, they believe something is inadequate in the component parts, whether that component is one's self or the other people you may be working with.

I saw this fixed mindset a lot with physicians who were chronically frustrated. If the operating room wasn't working well, they needed new staff. If the clinic wasn't working well, they needed a new manager. Their observations weren't always incorrect, but they tended to ascribe subpar performance with inadequate component parts—namely, their colleagues and teammates. Their mindsets were "fixed"; they lived in a world where only the swapping of parts, not learning how to understand and use those parts (including themselves), could create positive change. People with fixed mindsets do not see intelligence in themselves or others as mutable and changing. They are more likely to respond to feedback in a way that defends and upholds that fixed reality rather than embracing feedback as perspective that might help them see their way through to new insight. Consequently, they are more likely to seek validation and legitimation rather than helpful feedback, even when it's positively framed. Full disclosure, the universe *is* fixed in many ways, at least in our finite time frames. You can't make yourself taller by taking feedback well, applying learning, and "working on it." Nonetheless, people with a fixed mindset are less likely to see their own capability and that of others as "growable" and are at risk for diminished motivation in the face of new challenges. In a world full of unknowns and new challenges, the risk of fixed mindset thinking becomes clear.

On the other hand, I encountered a lot of physicians who possessed what Dweck calls a growth mindset. With the same staff, their operating room teams were humming along, learning from every case, getting better, adjusting positively to successes and setbacks equally, much like Brandon did with his young horses. People with a growth mindset tend to focus on effort and approach, rather than on end results. They tend to see any particular result as another clue in how to understand subsequent effort and approach. They see feedback as formative and helpful and actively seek it out. They may fail spectacularly, but they never let a failure go unharvested for key insights to equip themselves for the next try. Paradoxically, they create superior results in the long run, while developing resilience, adaptive approaches, and a self-identity as puzzle solvers and continuous learners, not as experts who have mastered a finite universe of knowledge. COVID-19, with its relentless attempts to infect people, jump into new environments, and mutate its own surface antigens, does not have a mindset in a literal sense. If it did, its mindset would clearly be growth. Biology in general, with its unceasing iteration of PLV toward growth and sustainable populations, relationships, and systems, essentially defines growth mindset in action.

Growth mindset is an essential condition for scaling PLV into the unknown of the VUCA world.

A growing body of research is showing that growth mindset can strengthen intrinsic motivation as well as effort and resilience.[1] Interestingly, gains in performance associated with mindset training in ninth graders showed that the effect was influenced heavily by peer norms. In other words, growth mindset itself requires social conditions, not just isolated effort, for its effect to flourish. As Dweck herself said, "Culture really matters."[2] Conditions in your epidemic can be mutually reinforcing.

At Microsoft, when Michael Bervell and the early starters of Growth Groups were just getting going, they actively used growth mindset as an originating condition and designed their pathogen's antigens (grit, vulnerability, 1 percent improvement, and giving) to set the conditions for attracting young people. The people in Growth Groups can be quite candid about other aspects of life in a big tech company, but in setting conditions, they chose to select corporate conditional elements that would add positive inertia to their efforts.

Microsoft CEO Sadya Nadella had already established growth mindset as a condition of Microsoft's future thinking, urging everyone to think about becoming a "learn it all culture," not a "know it all culture." Bervell and his colleagues set the stage for their epidemic by starting it in the context space of growth mindset and iterating off it. Further, they anchored the field effect of growth mindset in the leadership group that emerged as Growth Groups grew, continually welcoming new Growth Group leads to embody growth mindset, cultivate it in the group experiences, and use it to create feedback loops between groups. While Bervell and the early Growth Groups founders were intentional, they benefited from field effects beyond their control in the latent population of early-in-career colleagues who responded with such enthusiasm. One of the early founders of the Growth Groups epidemic at Microsoft told me he thought the conditions that spawned growth groups were "social starvation, growth mindset, curiosity, and the fact that it wasn't required and was a chance to explore."

We mentioned in Chapter 3 that complexity teems with complementary pairs. Epidemics arise in a world where stability and instability, freedom and limits, convergence and divergence are all happening simultaneously. You can see similar tensions in your work as people and companies struggle with centralization and decentralization, margin and meaning, conformity and disruption, innovation and optimization.

Your epidemic will have to navigate these tensions as well. If the people in your "infected population" can't leverage differences to continue to influence and be influenced by one another, you will see them gridlock in their work. The differences among them, which are normal and potentially advantageous to everyone's shared work, will break down into "either-or" entrenchment. People will take sides, avoid each other, attack each other, and fail to hear the value of perspectives that they see as opposing their own. Your epidemic, at best, will split into two opposing half-epidemics as either-or thinking organizes with antagonistic approaches around what could be a common and uniting idea.

In his 1992 book *Polarity Management: Identifying and Managing Unsolvable Problems*, Barry Johnson maps out an approach to leveraging these inevitable paired tensions, called polarities. He articulates a methodology for helping individuals and groups of all stripes maximize the upside "value pole" of each element of the dyad, while avoiding their respective downside "fear poles" (Figure 6.1). Done well, polarity thinking can help individuals and teams get "unstuck" and create new insights and performance. Polarity thinking is not the same as watered-down compromise or relativistic trade-off for the sake of expediency. The dialogue and thinking required shifts participants into new ways of thinking that open possibilities beyond their original perspectives. In essence, the polarity approach helps people create shared awareness of the best of both complements while avoiding the worst of both as well.

Such shifts are essential to the ideas of infection and contagion in social environments. Many of the participants in your positive epidemic will start out in very different places from one another around key polarities. Some may favor control, whereas others favor freedom. Some may favor predictability and certainty, whereas others prefer serendipity and surprise. For them to participate in exchanging and multiplying ideas and behaviors together, they will need to be able to hold their differences as attracting and uniting, rather than as repelling and dividing.

While simple behavior changes, such as choosing an Apple iPhone instead of another Samsung Galaxy, may not require much of a shift, more complex decisions and behavior patterns will. Truly internalizing a new idea, manifesting it in action, and thoughtfully engaging others with it is a complex act that requires each participant to see themselves in a paired way—as authors and creators and as receivers and acceptors. In a world with a lot of either-or, win-lose thinking and not-so-subtle struggles for social status, polarity thinking lowers the resistance to new ideas and flattens social hierarchies to allow every participant in an epidemic to speak with clarity and listen with humility. Polarity thinking decreases resistance and enhances the shifts in thinking, acting, and interacting that epidemics require.

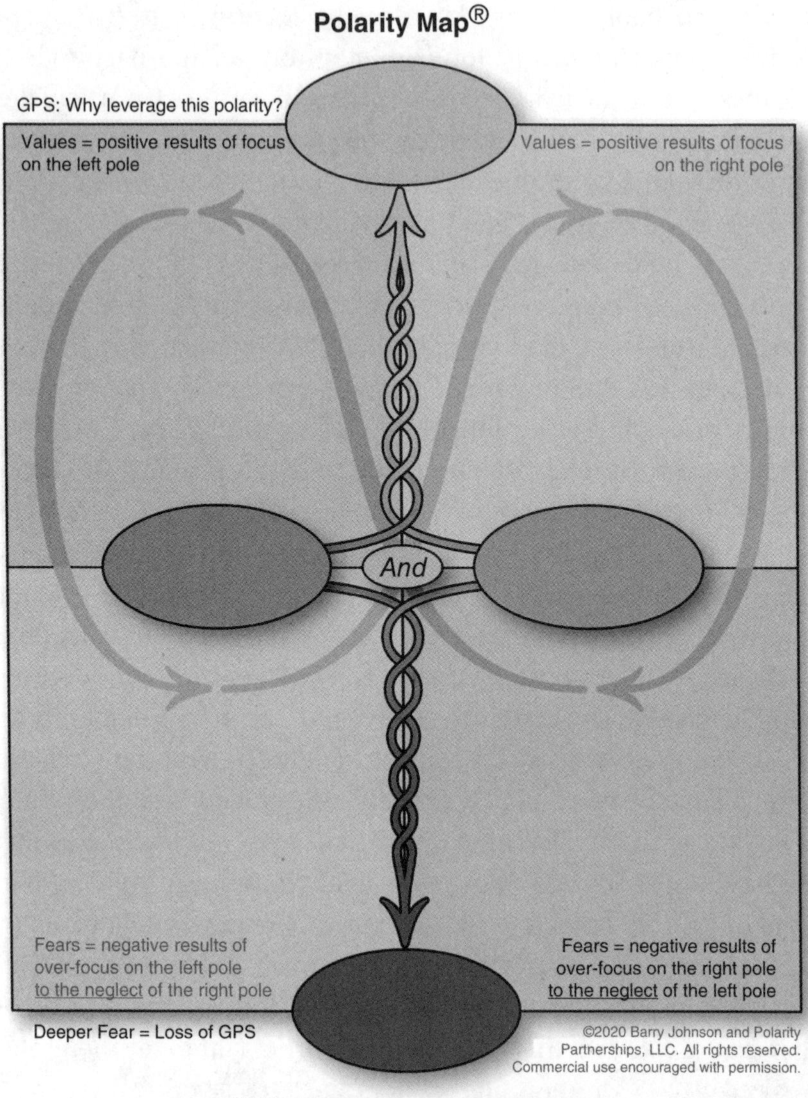

Figure 6.1: A generic polarity map ("GPS" = Greater Purpose Statement). Reprinted with permission from Polarity Partnerships.

Polarity Map® is a registered trademark of Barry Johnson & Polarity Partnerships, LLC. Commercial use encouraged with permission.

Both of these capacities—growth mindset and polarity thinking—lend themselves foundationally to how we think and perceive in a complex world. Of course, these constructs have to be converted to actions and then into defining patterns, but there is evidence that cultural values themselves, antecedent to behaviors, actually wire our brains.[3] Growth mindset helps us frame the results of our actions and perspectives so that we can iterate, adapt, and persevere relentlessly in the face of constantly changing conditions, including the responses of others. Polarities help us amplify our awareness of the value of complementary approaches, see wider alternatives, and anticipate the risk of over emphasis—all advantages in crafting the agility, awareness, and responsiveness of our positive epidemics.

Both conditions are worth grounding in any of your leadership efforts as you design epidemic action to scale PLV. Without these two gravitational fields, you risk the disorder of chaos or, more probably in our corporate and institutional environments, an inevitable tilt toward the rigidity of conformity and compliance as overplayed tendencies. In either case, the adaptive stability and spread of an epidemic cannot rise.

Spatial Conditions: Creating Space and Container

We all work in spatial conditions of some sort—roundpens, meeting rooms, warehouses, online video conferences. Other containers are the daily processes that structure our individual and shared work, processes like meetings, huddles, and presentations. All of these spaces are places where interaction and multiplication can happen and where mental fields like growth mindset, polarities, or inclusion can resonate. You will want to select such spaces where conditions can come together to increase the chance of infection with your thought pathogen and transmission of it between participants in those spaces.

Brandon works his horses in a roundpen of a particular size (radius 15 feet) because that design creates a condition, a container, that resonates with the other conditions he sets to optimize the interactions he creates with the horse. No matter how well he can work with a horse, doing it in a 100-foot pen or a square pen would create a different environment and training wouldn't go nearly as well. The roundpen works because it is both confining and liberating; the size and shape allow him to maximize that polarity. It also allows him to cue the animal and resonate with it physiologically without having to try to communicate across a larger distance, which would disrupt that signaling. Like COVID-19 transmission, in leadership epidemics, proximity matters.

In our work and lives, we are always moving through structures and processes. There are entry doors and exit doors, one-way streets and two-way ones. We have live face-to-face meetings and, increasingly, virtual ones (*camera on, camera off!*). Often we don't stop to think about how we are creating space and process that unleash epidemic thinking.

Consider the rooms pictured in Figures 6.2a and 6.2b. They are hundreds of miles apart but they bear very similar spatial characteristics. How are these spaces designed to enhance the simplicity, attraction, novelty, and dual purpose (the SAND pneumonic from Chapter 5) of a particular pathogen? How do they enhance learning, effort, motivation, both-and thinking, and the kind of ease we want to optimize the relational milieu that enhances neuroplasticity? When I ask

Figures 6.2a and 6.2b: Two boardrooms

people what happens in these rooms, they are fairly uniform in their response. "Edicts are passed down," or something to that effect, is what they describe.

The design of many of our rooms and processes often intertwines with more subtle nuances of social hierarchy, fixed mindsets, and either-or thinking. Too many rooms and processes minimize the chances for infection and contagion in favor of controlled inertial patterns. Interaction is often rote and sparse. Presentations and meetings often involve one person talking while many "listen," sometimes followed by a proscribed discussion or Q&A period. I've been in those rooms as presider and visitor. All too often what I saw was conforming thinking, one-way power gradients, unengaging interaction, and insufficient candor. More ironically, I have heard almost desperate exhortations for more original thinking, courage, new ideas, and willingness to change in rooms whose very design supports the opposite of the thinking and interacting necessary for such words to manifest in action.

Epidemics require contact. They require interface. Fortunately the rooms and processes of the average corporate workday can become much more effective containers with a little nudge from leaders. You can convert normal spaces and processes into novel spaces and processes that subtly shift the mindset cues and physiology in the room. Things begin to happen differently when people sit in different spots, stand instead of sit, move in and out of designed participative roles, put their phones away, or arrange themselves in open circles instead of closed tables. The following list offers examples of factors that can change the physical space around epidemic participants:

- Remove tables between participants.
- Gather in circles, not in rows or squares.
- Gather where there are windows and natural light.
- Change postures; stand and sit alternately.
- Rotate seating arrangements between and within meetings.
- Gather where observers can watch without interrupting.

- Put all phones and computers out of sight.
- Arrange seating so people can see each other face to face.

If you work in a place of poor general conditions, you may have to find smaller spaces where you can create positive niches and pockets. In Masese, the teachers and staff could not change things outside the school walls. They did want "creativity" to counter the idea of poverty as a state of nothing where there had once been something, and they wanted the students' experience with creativity to be both tangible and ultimately tied to larger dynamics of poverty in their community and country. They found their conditions—spaces, containers, fields—in each of their classrooms, in their schoolyard commons, in their daily morning assembly, in an extracurricular music program (which wasn't even going when I was first there) and in their computer lab.

They also decided to define a container around agriculture, a proud part of Uganda's historic abundance. Some of the American board members initially discouraged growing food as an educational emphasis, but the teachers and leadership team pointed out that the children lived in a community of poor nutrition and that Uganda had a long tradition of healthy local food (and two growing seasons per year, which made the Montana visitor envious!). Many of the teachers were from farming backgrounds as well. Linking creativity to growing food sounded like a wonderful idea as I heard it, but I did not imagine at the time how creating a mental container around the idea of creating food would translate to further physical spaces.

When I first saw the school, litter and trash drifted across the packed dirt of the inner courtyard. When I returned a year later, nearly all of the dusty yard, save a central space where the kids could play soccer, had been converted to committed soil plots rimmed with rock and brick and planted with cover crops, shrubs, and fruit trees. These spaces, in turn, had attracted young gardeners from the school classes who tended their plants daily. Figure 6.3 shows a before-and-after view of how creativity

Figure 6.3a: HELP primary schoolyard, 2018

flourished in the dual conditions of the schoolyard physical space and the mental frame of growing food.

You may not be able to define "big conditions" where you work; the teachers, staff, and students could not change Uganda's national unemployment or poverty rate, for example. However, epidemics always start small, so creating small spaces where conditions can create impact is a perfectly effective way to start your epidemic. When I first listened to the children and their dreams, no one mentioned being a farmer. When I returned and the creativity pathogen had wormed its

Figure 6.3b: HELP schoolyard after creativity began to flourish

way into the garden plots, several were thinking of making their living as farmers, and the headmaster of the school was well on her way to creating an agricultural innovation track. Conditions plus pathogen creates possibility.

Physiological Conditions: Setting the Stage for Relatedness

Advances in neuroscience tell us that the way we relate—internally with ourselves and externally with others in our environment—comes from and manifests itself in different brain states. In a mindful or "flow" state, the brain is best able to entertain new ideas, generate new action, form new habits, and fathom more possibilities. In fact, the term "open-minded" has a literal neural connotation. The brain is actually able to take in more and competing stimuli for consideration in open-minded states.[4]

In order to process and sift these multiple inputs, the brain has to slow down. In this state, the brain is neuroplastic—able to change its own patterns by creating new synapses and pruning off ones that are no longer helpful (no wonder it has to slow down—it's doing new construction and demolition at the same time!). We used to think the brain developed finitely as we formed in the womb and progressed through childhood to adulthood; we know now the brain is a far more dynamic organ, really a constantly evolving bio-electrical cloud of constant activity. Now neuroscientists are exploring the deeper mysteries of what causes shifts in and out of these states in real time and over longer periods of time. The brain in the mindful "flow" state releases more of the neurotransmitters *dopamine*, which causes a sense of empowerment; *serotonin*, which causes a sense of well-being; and *oxytocin,* which causes a feeling of closeness and trust.

We do know that the brain in a threat state, in an internal chemical environment high in the stress hormone cortisol, is not nearly as pliable and tends toward fight-flight-freeze mode. In this threatened state, our brains revert to the established patterns of our more reactive tendencies: assumptions, biases, current beliefs, rote actions. The more generative aspects of our brain are shut down in this state, making it much more difficult to learn—and encode in memory and action—new approaches.

You don't have to encounter freakish, life-threatening scenarios to trigger your brain into a fear state. In his 2008 article "SCARF: A Brain-Based Model for Collaborating with and Influencing Others," David Rock posits five domains—social status, certainty, autonomy, relatedness, and fairness—whose circumstances ease our minds or trigger our brains into a threat posture.[5] Any of these factors can themselves be overt or very subtle. Walking into an unknown conversation with your boss, who has a history of telling you what to do without listening to you, can rouse the feelings of inferior social status, uncertainty, lost autonomy, a bad relationship, and unfairness all at once within a few seconds. Going through a divorce or a fallout with long-time friends or having a political argument with your family can all send your brain into a state of threat. Although we may not think of these things as painful, and they may not be five-alarm screaming events, the region that lights up on brain scans in this state is the same region that lights up in response to physical pain.[6]

From years of observation, Brandon understood how a threatened brain could block his horses' ability to create trust, learn new skills, and build cooperative habits. As prey animals, horses are quick to go to flight, and their bodies show it. Away from a herd and alone in a pen where they have to encounter the uncertainty of new learning and the ambiguity of what Brandon calls their dominance status, the roundpen is a potential container for triggering a threat response for an animal that lives in wide-open space. He countered that tendency by shifting his own state to one of peaceful calm, which flowed into his voice and movements. This more mindful, attentive state—when we are most capable of learning, reflecting, and understanding—works at a slower pace than our fast, reactive brain, and it requires focused attention and lack of distraction as it entertains new and varied concepts. The slow brain does not work by accident; it needs space.

A horse isn't a light switch any more than a human being is, but starting with very little else, Brandon's restful physiology caused a similar shift in the horse. (We now know there is such a thing as brain-to-brain communication outside of language,[7] but even without such capability, a horse naturally reads our body language, and we humans read one another's as well.) Subsequent connective signals to and within the horse—affirmation for effort, clarity of role with Brandon, the opportunity to make choices, and an increasing sense of connection between human and horse—all built on this initial physiological state and deepened the bonding so needed by the animal with Brandon as the work continued. Watching Brandon and the horse drove home one of my most powerful leadership lessons: *start with physiology*.

I found it worked at the bedside also, where I was continually meeting people whose circumstances had fired up their threat response even before they arrived in a strange environment to meet a strange person, me, while they were lying on their backs, uncertain of what was next for them. Time might have been of the essence and pain with real risk to life and limb were often in the room, but slowing things down and connecting with a patient never failed. Over the years, several took the time later to mention how helpful it was to them when their neurons were racing, including a colleague who died shortly after he and I found ourselves tragically paired as doctor and patient.

We don't have to stretch our imagination to understand how our work and civic environments are full of threat-state triggers. Just having our political beliefs countered can send us into a powerful defense response.[8] Disagreements at work, uncertainty about how projects will go or how our perspectives will be heard, and working with new material or people can all trigger our protective "threat brain." As you lead your epidemic, you won't be able to mitigate all the minithreats that everyone feels, and you will want to cultivate the capacity for people to shift into a state of "alert ease," "flow," or mindfulness whenever the situation calls for it.

The brain's physiological state can be a powerful condition for facilitating this capacity. Potentiating people's ability to think in terms of growth mindset or both-and polarities, both individually and across the individuals in a shared experience like a conversation or a collaborative effort, can set the stage for their willingness and ability to do so. Grounding the "physiology field" can create powerful context for the processes of infection and contagion. Ideas that magnify fear and threat infect and spread quite well in threat-posture populations and are often waved like flags of agitation by public figures, but our role as leaders is more thoughtful. We are creating epidemics of performance, learning, and vitality, not clouds of reactivity, bias, and neural duress.

When we pay close attention to ourselves as individuals or as groups, we will often catch ourselves in a reactive physiological state, triggered by our environment. Although we can't always change the circumstances that prompted our neural state, we humans have the ability to change our physiological state willfully, and we can learn it. We can essentially put ourselves in a neuroplastic state. Mindfulness is essentially intentional neuroplasticity. Beyond the funky neuroscience (which is really cool), we know now that we can create these conditions internally and among people as they relate. Actions such as learning a new language, creating art, or doing tasks with your nondominant hand can all support a more neuroplastic brain state.[9] As neuroscientists say, "The neurons that fire together wire together." This individual and group self-modulation of neural state is the closest thing to a leadership miracle in terms of setting conditions. The subsequent interaction and multiplication of your epidemic will build off the "field" or "container" of these neural conditions.

Like Brandon's focus on listening to the horse, creating conditions involves paying close attention to what is needed in a local environment. Entering Memorial Health System in 2008 as a newcomer, I had a strong sense that our positive pathogen would need to be trust if we were to counter such widespread chronic proliferative dysphoria, as I had named our collective disease on my whiteboard. I had heard thousands of health care people describe the value of trust and the cost of its absence over the previous 10 years. As technical people, they didn't usually put it that way, but when they started to describe their best team experience and their worst team experiences in small conversations, clear trends emerged from the varied details and unique stories. First, PLV clearly emanated from best team experience, and PLV clearly eroded in worst team experiences. Four themes also emerged, every single time. Those themes were "being on the same page" or "common ground"; "having conversations we needed to have, the way we needed to have them, when we need to have them"; "every voice counted, we all had something to contribute, answers came from everywhere"; and finally, "we trusted each other."

I could have guessed correctly that the same phenomenon would hold in my new organization. After all, people are people, and health care team experiences have the same elements everywhere. I had also asked people in the hallways and forums for a few weeks what rules had guided the organization to its present state, the one that I identified as chronic proliferative dysphoria on my whiteboard. I had explained to people I met that as an emergency physician, I highly valued the chance to listen during my "30 seconds to meaningful rapport," and I wanted to know what unspoken rules had driven how people thought, acted, and interacted.

As an entering executive, I was just getting to know a population of people who were mistrustful of each other and of leaders in general because of what they viewed as "special deals for special people." Further, the economy was under duress, a lot of our employees had spouses who were losing their jobs, and the jockeying for position after the CEO transition that put me in my role were all creating a kind of collective threat response. Our brains were not at neuroplastic ease. Although I was optimistic about the future, I didn't think declaring a new pathogen unilaterally from on high would do anything but increase the immune system *against* a new rule from an outsider, no matter how healthy I might have hoped that signal might be. There was just too much distrust. I also wasn't about to leave the selection of a healthy pathogen to chance in a stressed social environment that was perfectly situated to perpetuate old patterns rather than originate new ones.

Rather than talk about growth mindset or polarities, we created a series of experiences to allow people to reflect on their experiences in the organization and name what worked and what didn't. We gathered about three hundred leaders and opinion influencers in a big ball room for a two-day retreat, including board members, physicians, organizational line leadership, and a couple of city council members.

People had had a chance to share with each other their own stories of worst team experiences and best team experiences. After they had considered the common elements that supported their aspirations or resulted in historic frustrations and dashed dreams, they had identified the same four themes I had heard in countless other environments. Together, they identified key elements of trust as a cornerstone of our future. We called it The Trust Cycle (Figure 6.4), and it became the pathogen for our subsequent four years of epidemic action.

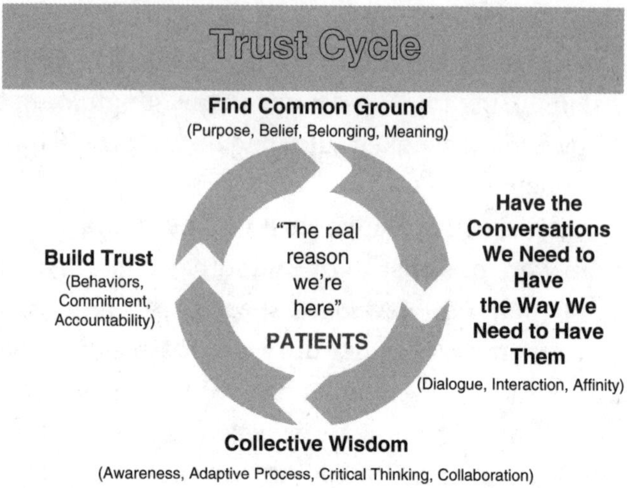

Figure 6.4: The Trust Cycle

If we hadn't created the conditions that allowed people to express their own experiences, name their aspirations, and vent their frustrations and then see those as patterns they had built and could change, I don't think I could have ever convinced them we needed to start with trust. In essence, we created a container to allow our pathogen to emerge directly from people's shared experience. Creating conditions is one of the first steps in putting a pathogen on the move, but leaders can also create conditions to *form* pathogens, interactions, and multipliers as well. The key is to understand what conditions are already in the environment and how they encourage or oppose infection and contagion in your population.

At Memorial, we had a lot of negative conditions that undermined our teams' ability to perform, to try new and better approaches, to energize our work. In the several weeks I spent asking people what the "rules of the road" were in our health care organization, the list I got from several hundred people was notable. I hadn't asked for *bad* rules, but the list I wrote down was enough to discourage anyone. Those rules formed a sort of conditional gray cloud in the organization.

These "old rules" did not strike anyone as the conditions for a better day. When I asked people if these rules created the conditions that allowed us to reach the fulfillment of our personal and organizational purpose, their response was a clear "No." Looking back, I made a mistake in how I asked. I should have framed my curiosity with an acknowledgment that I was seeking positive and helpful rules as well as negative and harmful ones. Because I didn't do that and instead asked the question without its own "formative condition," the mood of the place flowed forth in a negative list that later had its own dispiriting effect.

The old rules were the conditions that had fostered the current state of poor performance, stagnant learning, and degraded vitality, and we needed new conditions. Once people were intentional about creating trust, we created another series of experiences asking people what the rules could be if we converted the old rules to new ones (Table 6.1). We had a lot of work to do to go from defining "new rules" to living by new patterns of thinking, acting, and interacting, but we had effectively set a field for the future and a container for daily action.

At Microsoft, Michael Bervell and the early Growth Groups prototypers took advantage of the open space to create conditions that allowed "best friend at work" and professional development to begin to flourish. They started with a community-building get-together and then split people into standing groups—smaller "containers"—of 10–15 people. The size of groups, however permanent or temporary they are, is important. We all know we feel differently among one or two people than we do among thousands, and research shows there is an ideal size of five to eight participants for small groups.[10]

Bervell had already "preplanted" conditions in his antigens, which helped the early group lead work within that context. Growth Groups also defined conditions by having a defined interval, enough structure that people could see what they were getting into, and continuous experimentation around what attendees enjoyed and what kept bringing them back. They measured these things, as you would expect

Table 6.1: Old Rules and New Rules at Memorial Health System, 2008–2009

Old Rules	New Rules
■ The King says	■ Our commitment compels
■ Command & Control	■ Catch & Release
■ Competition	■ Collaboration
■ Manage our physicians	■ Lead with physicians
■ Employees just don't understand—give part of picture	■ Employees are our wisdom; create the complete picture
■ If I'm not there, I don't count	■ Nothing about me, without me
■ Build your defensible empire	■ Build high-performance team
■ Complain about the problem	■ Cultivate the solutions
■ Deal before real	■ Relationships before deals
■ Do what you're told; don't ask questions	■ Ask questions—explore and seek to understand
■ Lead with a bunker mentality	■ Leaders are visible, teaching, learning
■ Think about how it used to be	■ Build future
■ Secrets	■ Transparency
■ Manage day to day	■ Plan and perform long term
■ Silo decision-making	■ Free flow of information
■ Finance vs. quality	■ Quality drives finance
■ No margin, no mission	■ Margin through mission
■ Loyalty rewarded above all things	■ Commitment to mission
■ Nurse-centric	■ Patient-centric
■ Expediency	■ Accountability
■ *"Thank you for your input but we're doing it my way"*	■ *"Your input has helped us find a better way"*
■ *"Fire, aim, ready"*	■ *"Ready, aim, fire"*
■ Here's what's wrong	■ Create what's right
■ Unfunded mandates	■ Disciplined decisions
■ Hospital	■ System
■ We're the best	■ We work to improve every day
■ Physician-driven	■ Physician-led
■ Compete for shrinking pie/scarcity	■ Collaborate and grow the pie/abundance
■ We can't change	■ We can and will change
■ Tolerate poor performance	■ Teach, learn, perform
■ Vengeance and retaliation	■ Understanding and collaboration
■ Tolerance of bad behavior/poor performance	■ Building good behavior/high performance
■ Physicians as "necessary evil"	■ Physicians as leaders and partners
■ Tribal warfare	■ Community building
■ Inquisition and criticism	■ Inquiry and curiosity
■ Black & White/binary	■ Color/multifaceted

tech engineers to do, by a surveyed net promoter score, which started and stayed above 50 (a net promoter score of 50 is good), even as the groups themselves went virtual when the pandemic imposed its own conditions in early 2020. Further, they set the curricular conditions along their first 12-week cohort with a lot of structure for the first three weeks and, intentionally, a lot of room to experiment during the last nine weeks. “The first conversation is always the hardest, right?” said Aly Mirza, one of the early prototypers. The Growth Groups founders accordingly made things easy and undemanding for the first three weeks, betting on the collective energy and creativity of the groups to self-organize the remainder of the time within the more flexible conditions.

Was Microsoft, the big corporate entity, surprised by the emergence of Growth Groups? Yes and no. Kareem Choudhry, the Corporate Vice President of Gaming, was pleasantly surprised when his chief of staff picked the invitational email from the Growth Group founders. “Microsoft created this primordial stew. Growth Groups was not an accident.” He went on to cite Microsoft’s intentional and formal commitment to growth mindset and its efforts to hire entrepreneurial, self-starting new hires with an action bias. Although Growth Groups per se wasn’t predictable, *something* like Growth Groups was bound to emerge when you create the ”primordial stew” of conditions that favor epidemics.

Conditions create both freedom functions and boundary functions, and Growth Groups’ originating conditions serve as a good example of yet another polarity in that regard (as they linked corporate imperative with individual need, structured time frame and curriculum with freedom to create the last nine weeks). Like Brandon’s roundpen, conditions create both the space and the limits that invite people into the ease that will enable them to take on the edge and novelty of new ideas. In any environment where people lead, follow, and organize, there are innumerable ways to define the fields and containers which will enhance—or inhibit—the social infection and contagion you're hoping to cultivate. Like the young early-in-career people at Microsoft, you can create your own conditions and keep improvising as people respond.

Handily—and in keeping with the interdependence of complex systems—conditions are also reflexive with interactions and multipliers. If you have enough people in growth mindset and the right state of ease, for example, they each create a little field effect of their own back into the system, and thus create a mini multiplier effect and nudge people toward interaction patterns. As a result, you will see new containers pop up spontaneously as people resonate with the conditions in your environment. At Memorial, after we had anchored the idea of new rules as a vehicle for creating trust, one of our largest units, our neonatal intensive care group, stepped forward and volunteered to get to work first on these principles. They were a poorly performing and dispirited unit and went on—rapidly—to become one of the healthiest examples of "new rules" in our organization, and their PLV proved it. Once they got going, other units became curious, and we had to scramble to match them (and learn from them) with the interaction design we will discuss in the next chapter.

People get to choose their response, of course, but setting and sustaining healthy conditions multiplies the chances of both intentional and serendipitous action. To create an epidemic, you don't need everyone to respond all at once or even the same way. You do need those spaces, containers, and fields that continually support pathogen viability and spread via tiny shifts in how people think, feel, and interact. One of my financial colleagues used to say, "You can't fatten a cow by weighing it." His point was that sometimes leaders spend too much time checking on results and not enough time setting conditions for those results. As leaders, we have powerful leverage in creating conditions, and those conditions can spawn unexpected yield, just as good soil can drive abundant harvest.

In our work settings, we tend to spend a lot of time on the "what"—what we're going to get done, what we did, how much and how little.

Because P = Performance is important, we have organized our thinking and action around tasks and results. To convene an epidemic that has effect, staying power and adaptivity, one that energizes people with the vitality to keep creating its effects as well as start others, we have to spend time on *how we respond and relate*. How leaders relate directly in small settings, and how we tie our own words and behavior to the cognitive, spatial, and physiological conditions that optimize how humans exchange, adopt, and translate ideas into action will be well worth your time. Pick your mindsets, pick your spaces, and find your ways to create ease amid duress, and wherever people gather, they will be more ready to move.[11]

Notes

1. David S. Yeager et al., "Mindsets That Promote Resilience: When Students Believe That Personal Characteristics Can Be Developed," *Educational Psychologist* 47, no. 4 (October 19, 2012): 302–314, https://doi.org/10.1080/00461520.2012.722805.
2. Carol S. Dweck, "Brainology: Transforming Students' Motivation to Learn," National Association of Independent Schools, Winter 2008, https://www.nais.org/magazine/independent-school/winter-2008/brainology/.
3. Marianna Pogosyan, "How Culture Wires Our Brains," *Psychology Today,* January 6, 2017, https://www.psychologytoday.com/us/blog/between-cultures/201701/how-culture-wires-our-brains.
4. Luke Smillie, "Openness to Experience: The Gates of the Mind," *Scientific American,* August 15, 2017, https://www.scientificamerican.com/article/openness-to-experience-the-gates-of-the-mind/.
5. David Rock, "SCARF: A Brain-Based Model for Collaborating with and Influencing Others," *Neuroleadership Journal* 1 (2008): 1–8, https://web.archive.org/web/20100705024057/http://www.your-brain-at-work.com/files/NLJ_SCARFUS.pdf.
6. David Rock, "Managing with the Brain in Mind," *Strategy+Business* Autumn 2009, no. 56 (August 27, 2009), http://laspositascollege.

edu/gv/pdc/assets/docs/mandatoryflex/archives/fall2018/WTArticle.pdf.

7. Robert Martone, "Scientists Demonstrate Direct Brain-to-Brain Communication in Humans," *Scientific American,* October 29, 2019, https://www.scientificamerican.com/article/scientists-demonstrate-direct-brain-to-brain-communication-in-humans/.
8. Robert Rosenkranz, "The Neuroscience of Open-Mindedness Related to Political Views," Rosenkranz Remarks: The Blog of Robert Rosenkranz, February 9, 2017, http://robertrosenkranz.com/neuroscience-open-mindedness/.
9. Courtney E. Ackerman, MA, "What Is Neuroplasticity? A Psychologist Explains," PositivePsychology.com, accessed April 6, 2021, https://positivepsychology.com/neuroplasticity/.
10. Janet Choi, "Why Jeff Bezos' Two-Pizza Team Rule Still Holds True in 2018," I Done This Blog, December 4, 2018, http://blog.idonethis.com/two-pizza-team/.
11. Jeffrey R. Young, "New Study Shows Where 'Growth Mindset' Training Works (and Where It Doesn't)," *EdSurge*, August 7, 2019, https://www.edsurge.com/news/2019-08-07-new-study-shows-where-growth-mindset-training-works-and-where-it-doesn-t.

7 Designing Interaction

No one obsesses about microstructure.

—Keith McCandless, Liberating Structures

In the universe, big things arise out of little things piling up and bumping into each other. Sometimes, you just get bigger piles of little things and nothing more. Lots of sand grains stacked next to each other add up to beaches and sand piles. Lots of salt crystals give you big piles of salt. Sometimes though, you get things that surprise and inspire beyond the aggregation of those little things. These surprises are the miracle of emergence and transformation from self-organization, the rise of powerful macro effects from the bubbling of tiny interactions that may themselves seem so trivial. The design and sifting of these tiny interactions is where the potential of an epidemic's conditions and pathogen become the reality of epidemic action.

The Power of Cellular Processes

When lots of living cells pile up, you get an organism with properties consistent with, and yet beyond, the mere clumping of cells. Once, each of us was a unique single-celled organism bobbing in the space-container of our mother's uterus and its originating conditions of temperature, oxygen, glucose, and a thousand other nuances of metabolic brine. Our DNA source code, the one for our eye color, facial shape, heart and lung structure, our hair color and body length, even significant parts of our personality, was wrapped in the 23 pairs of chromosomes in the nucleus of that one cell. The code itself, really a person-a-gen, resulted from the union of two cells with only a half-code's worth of DNA, each one an incomplete and random toss-in donated from our mother and father from their respective reservoirs of germinal cells called gametes.

Months later, years later, decades later, endlessly until we die, the symphony of cells that is each of us runs on the unceasing interplay of interaction between cells and the conditions that support them in the larger container of the body. Emergence—that magical "beyond the sum of parts" quality of complex adaptivity—defines us. We have plans, thoughts, consciousness. We dream, despair, respond, reflect, imagine, innovate. All of those things—*all* of those things—depend on the summation of billions of tiny interactions running relentlessly and continuously within and between our cells. At our start and at our end, we are the summation of incomplete particles swarming into completeness, never done.

We don't spend much time thinking about our cells, most of us, but if they go down, we go down. In a condition called sepsis, a catastrophic unwinding of bodily integrity caused by infection, our blood pressure drops, our kidneys and heart fail, our blood becomes more acidic, our brains stop working, and our lungs cannot keep up with the need to expel waste carbon dioxide and take in enough oxygen. At the bedside in an ICU, we are barely recognizable. We lie bloated and motionless on our back, hooked to a breathing machine with tubes in our nose, mouth, veins, and bladder as we spiral down. It's a dramatic look, and it's a dramatic and often lethal collapse.

Beyond all the macro effects you can see from the bedside, the implosion is really a massively scaled failure at the cellular level. Intracellular and intercellular interactions, the tiny processes that ensure stable function, adjustment, and metabolism—PLV at the cellular level—have crashed. Only when these processes are restored again will we reemerge with our thoughts, our dreams, our reflections, and our insights. If the person lying in that ICU bed is an Olympic athlete, the idea of a gold medal may hang in well wishes above the bed, but the notion of training for that moment, dreaming of that moment, let alone competing in it, is folly until the function of tiny cells is restored. The fundamental unit of the body is the cell. We forget, but it is always true.

Just as most of us go about our lives paying very little attention to the integrity and impact of our cellular PLV, leaders often forget about the mathematical power of all those tiny interactions between people going on in an organization. The organizational charts, proscribed protocols, defined decision-making processes, and specified key performance indicators (KPIs) and objectives and key results (OKRs) of formal organizational activity lull us into a sense of operational reality, when reality is actually a vast, seething cloud of innumerable and tiny interactions. Shift interaction, and you can shift the outcome of those interactions. Multiply the interaction patterns from small to big, and you shift the behavior of your organization. None of these small interactions approach totality in themselves, but they set the stage for it.

In 2010, we brought Keith McCandless and Henri Lipmanowicz in to help our IT team at Memorial. Keith and Henri had prior corporate careers but had created a powerful approach for creating systemic shifts in human systems via their "liberating structures" approach (`liberatingstrutures.com`). Some time prior to Keith and Henri's arrival, the IT team had identified their "old rules" persona as "we're the people who tell you what you can't have." They had historically expressed that pathogen with vigor. Our CIO, Dr. Jonathan Velez, described them as "blinded by their rightness." Positively, they had also defined their "new rules" identity as "giving you the information you need the way you need it, when you need it." In the setting of our larger organizational emphasis on trust, they had made an intentional shift of pathogens, but they had an interaction problem. Their patterns were crusty and off-putting. They needed and wanted to change their patterns of thinking and acting, but they weren't sure how to do so. As Velez said at the time, "We know where we need to end up, but we need smiling people ready to keep going, not guerilla resistance or ashes where people once stood."

We created a two-day workshop container, and each IT team member was asked to invite a non-IT stakeholder with whom they worked on a regular basis. Three hundred people of our various tribes gathered in a single large room, half from IT and half from nursing, quality, pharmacy, revenue cycle, compliance, laboratory, and facilities. Throughout the two days, people broke into dyads and triads, convened into larger debriefs, scattered again into different small combinations. They sat in small groups and stood in circles; They talked, listened, asked questions, laughed, and pondered. The energy in the room oscillated from laughter to quiet disclosure, from whimsy to vulnerability.

The IT team went on to improve their working relationships across departments considerably and rapidly, saving us over three million dollars a year in wasted rework and interdepartmental friction. It didn't happen all in those two days, but what did happen was an awareness on the part of several hundred people that is true in any population: by redefining their patterns of interaction, they could redefine patterns of results and impact. Dr. Velez has since gone on to two other leadership roles in health care, creating abundant results in both, and is the frequent recipient of the question, "Can you show me how you get that to happen?"

What emerges from the micro-interactions Keith and Henri design through their work is as sophisticated and infectious as it is simple and practical. Common identity, variable experiences, and original insights all bubble out of the small conversations and harmonize in the larger room and in the larger group. Wide authorship and participation distills into commitment that is strongly held, supportive of the larger organization but, at the same time, highly textured and individually attractive. As Keith says, "In any given work, not everyone will get it, but someone, *someone*, will always get it, and then *everyone* will get it."

In an article by Keith and his colleague Fisher Qua called "More Magic, Less Mystery," Keith and Fisher observe that by "paying close attention to the composition of micro-organizing elements, it becomes possible to design interaction with a high degree of variability at the micro-scale (experienced as imaginative play) while retaining metastability at the macro-scale (experienced as creative or useful results)."[1] In other words, their approach produces the variability and stability so essential to organizational and institutional function in complex environments. People find coherence in shared action and freedom—even delight—in their individual participation. It's a handy thing to spin up if you are leading for PLV at scale.

Ideally, micro-interactions should be universal and applicable in any and all pieces of work and wherever people bump into each other. COVID-19 flourished wherever people gathered a certain way, independent of what they were doing at the time. Choral singers, auto mechanics, meat packers, athletes, college students, restaurant patrons, partygoers, and politicians all contracted it. What people were doing at the time was secondary to how they interacted. Leading an epidemic means fashioning similar patterns of interaction that can move wherever people gather and whatever their technical jobs are in the spaces and containers where they work and mix.

Neuroscience tells us that we can expect people to respond certain ways under certain conditions. Complexity being what it is, full of unpredictability, and humans being what they are, similar and unique, means that leaders can facilitate patterns but cannot predict exactly how any one event will occur or how any one person will respond (this is a good thing!).

Like Microsoft, you can create the "primordial stew" that Kareem Choudhry recognizes and trusts, and you can predict good things will pop up, but you cannot ordain precisely how or when. Accordingly, your role as a leader becomes vastly more generative when you help create interaction patterns rather than try to control behaviors. Like Brandon's horses and in far deeper dimensions, people get to choose.

No amount of coercion can take that away or ever be healthy. Creating the conditions for freedom within these interactions is essential at the practical and ethical levels.

While humans choose how we respond and participate, with more or less awareness of our own neural state at the time, we are also highly influenced by social context and the thoughts and behaviors of those we trust. As parents, we want our children to spend time with healthy peers and mentors, and for good reason. People influence and are influenced by one another, no matter how freely we are able to decide for ourselves from a jurisdictional perspective. Beyond the intuitive comfort we have with these notions, the research itself can be quite shocking. Network research shows that we are influenced in our thinking and actions by people three levels of network connection away from us—people we don't even know![2]

We need both these things—individual volition and social influence—in teams and organizations. Pouring them over your organization from on high, proclaiming them from a single point source, rolling them out, driving them down, and cascading by hierarchical authority and policy mandate will work about as well as masks mandates did. Leaders cannot change these fundamental realities in any case: people *are* influenced, they *do* decide, they *do* think well and poorly. The best odds for spawning widespread positive disease rise from the ground up, which doesn't mean you shouldn't be thinking of the benefits of leading top down. Microsoft necessarily and effectively set the conditions for growth mindset from the very top, from CEO Sadya Nadella. The manifestation of Growth Groups into a 2,000-person epidemic of engaged and connected new hires necessarily and effectively rose from the ground up.

Pathogens and conditions are essential for epidemics, but interaction combusts these elements into infection and contagion. Interactions are the flywheel that shifts an epidemic from incipient "might happen" to present and moving "here we go." Interaction literally means "action between," and organizations and teams are swimming with it. Interactions are where antigen meets receptor, where the diseased person showers the next candidate for infection with more pathogen load than the new host's immune system can handle, where two people create what neither could separately. Interaction is where active participation begins. These interactions are the conveyors of your epidemic; define them well, and multiply them, and PLV can scale. Once you've got a pathogen bubbling in the right conditions and you have picked out a few spaces as containers, it's time to get intentional about designing interactions that favor uptake and spread.

Despite the massive inertia of interaction patterns, leaders often take interaction itself for granted or fail to notice its implications. I hosted a webinar with health care executives in 2018 on designing systemic resilience—strategic, operational, and cultural—in organizations. I polled the participants on whether they focused on results. One hundred percent of respondents said yes. I asked how many of them designed processes to deliver those results. One hundred percent of respondents said yes. I asked how many focused on creating conditions for PLV, and 10 percent said yes. I asked how many of the organizations had an executive focus on designing patterns of interactions, and zero percent said yes.

It's not that we don't pay attention to how we ourselves or even others interact. Most leaders are developed and acculturated to focus on how we think, act, and interact, which makes common sense. It's where we have the greatest control and self-assertion. The leverage in a population, though, is in its patterns of interaction, not in the aberrancies, however positive, of a single leader or participant. Individual interactions cannot match the power of patterns of interactions.

You might be infected and contagious, but you're not exponential until you're designing interaction patterns whose impact on infection and contagion recruit increasing numbers of positive disease makers. Having been a CEO, I can vouch for the CEOs out there when I say that no matter how good I am, how perfect I am in every thought and encounter (and I'm not and neither are any other CEOs), I am only one particle, and I can only bump into so many people directly. I may be graced with social and hierarchical authority, but I still lose the math.

As Kareem Choudhry at Microsoft observes, "I can work to create a phenomenal experience within my bubble, but my blast radius is only a certain size." That from a skilled executive with a big bubble running one of Microsoft's business units.

Consider a patient who goes through a hospital for a procedure. By the time the patient enters the front door and leaves for home, the patient may encounter a hundred people. If one is kind and the others are merely busy, the patient won't describe the experience or the place as kind. The patient may remember the kind person or the kind gesture, but the overall impression will be "They were too busy to worry about me." The sum total of the interactions is what defines reality.

Given that there are millions of them in an organization, what is the value of an interaction? On the scale of things, not very much. A given interaction could be negative, have no value at all (in which case the interaction is a waste of time), or be positive. The pattern, potentially replicable across that larger number, however, is powerful. If you are trying to create an epidemic of PLV moving through patterns of thought, action, and interaction, intense focus on the value of interaction parameters is worth your while. The stimulation of thought, action, and interaction to create a tiny and contagious burst of PLV *every time, with anyone, on any topic,* is where the potential of your pathogen and conditions blossoms into effect. It may be small, but now it's real and capable of moving.

Like the executives on the webinar, many of us don't think about designing patterns of interaction, but we do design and reinforce all sorts of elaborate processes (meetings, policies, protocols) whose role paradoxically serves to limit interaction and control behavior. When we think about the effect such design has on motivation—remember mastery/improvement, autonomy–volition, and purpose–connection?—it's impressive how dogged people are at staying with the work an organization needs them to do! Nonetheless, the design of the modern workplace is exacting a high toll. Perhaps if we optimize thinking, acting, interacting as a cellular unit of larger patterns, we wouldn't see the widespread burnout and disengagement we do see.

If you wanted to design the COVID-19 epidemic, you would have done well to put people in small spaces and orchestrate the things that cause viral transmission from person to person. You would want people to cough on each other, speak just inches from each other's faces, and repeat those kinds of interactions over and over again. Internally, you would want to make sure the virus landed in just the right spots to hook onto the right kind of receptors on the right kind of cells and were interacting with the right cellular processes to cause both disease and viral multiplication. You would want to design effective collisions between pathogen and host to enhance infection and between infected and uninfected hosts to drive contagion.

In practical terms, the principles that undergird infectious and contagious interaction are the things we learned from our kindergarten teachers, favorite mentors, grandparents, and old cliches, but a growing body of neuroscience is validating how they work. In her work on conversational intelligence, the late Judith Glaser called them rituals.[3] Others have called them organizational routines.[4] Glenda Eoyang, my original muse on self-organization, called them collisions and now calls them exchanges. Whatever you name them, interaction rules are the simple parameters that guide how we give and take in conversation and relationship with others. They are the simple norms that, to riff off Keith McCandless and Henri Lipmanowicz, structure how we collide with other people and liberate our thoughts and actions to deeper levels of efficacy. They are an organization's cellular processes, and as they go, the body will go.

Principles of Infectious and Contagious Interaction Design

Numerous common elements in our internal and external environment can throw us into a threat state and render the brain resistant to new ideas, creating a sort of "neural immune system." Such a brain state becomes antagonistic to any epidemic except ones that traffic in a threatened state—epidemics of defensiveness, aggression, or denial. We have plenty of those. David Rock's SCARF model discussed in Chapter 6 (status, certainty, autonomy, relatedness, and fairness) frames the domains our brains constantly monitor for potential threats that have direct implications on how we can design interaction.

In effect, Rock explains why the stable patterns of culture eat the hoped-for new patterns required by strategy and everything else for lunch. To the always-scanning brain, a normal human day comes with repeated challenges to these five elements of "brain ease," so the social milieu that multiplies or mitigates these threats has a huge impact on how individuals and groups interact in real time. As we pointed out with regard to conditions, if you hit these danger buttons in a social environment, the experience causes the brain to light up in the same region where it perceives physical pain.[5] The implications are clear. Design interactions the wrong way, and you'll be asking people to work into neural pain. Small gestures, comments, and circumstances can have hidden and cumulative effects on how teams think, act, and perform.

Fortunately, we can also define interaction so that our brains, individually and together, resonate into that more generative state, the one where possibility, analysis, insight, and attention all improve. Moreover, those kinds of conversations are attractive—we gain value from them and want to try again. We may not be able to predict what might happen a hundred conversations down the line, but we don't need to know. We just need to be ready for the next one, and a little bit better at PLV coming out of one and heading into the next.

ACE Interaction

Ideal interaction designs can work anywhere, anytime, with any combination of people, universal to humans and subsequently adapted to culture but not determined by it. The pneumonic, ACE, where A = affirmation/appreciation, C = Curiosity, and E = Empathy, defines three universally relational principles. These principles can be modeled by way of personal example or designed into interaction rules for use in any topic, including difficult ones. ACE is the antidote to threats to SCARF. The three elements of affirmation/appreciation, curiosity, and empathy do not prevent threats to our status, certainty, autonomy, relatedness, or fairness—there will always be those, real or perceived. They do afford neural and behavioral guidance to how we can interact under conditions where we might shut down.

A = Affirmation/Appreciation

Numerous studies link the impact of affirmation and appreciation, or gratitude, with shifts in the human brain and performance. We often say that four or five positive cues to every corrective one is the ideal ratio for coaching, learning, and development.[6] Just *hearing* positive words can create a positive physical response.[7] Self-affirmation itself reduces stress, and affirmation lights up the same brain center that activates whenever stress decreases.[8]

In addition to lighting up our brain's reward centers and unleashing the powerful effects of the neurotransmitter dopamine (the same flush of which causes euphoria in cocaine users), affirmation has a positive correlation with creating future goals and predicted change in sedentary behavior.[9] Think about that: merely hearing affirmation from one's self or others can impact how we create goals and move from sitting still to moving forward. In learning new procedures, positive feedback to surgeons significantly improved performance speed from the first attempt to the second attempt, 39 seconds to 4 seconds, respectively, for those who received positive feedback versus those who did not, for a roughly two-and-a-half minute procedure.[10] That's an improvement of 25 percent over affirmation alone.

Affirmation's near cousin, appreciation or gratitude, has similar positive brain effects. In functional MRI scanning, when researchers inspect the brain visually while subjects practice a particular emotion, gratitude showed activity in moral cognition and reward centers.[11] In other words, participants were both more at ease and more aware of "the right thing to do." In another study, subjects who participated in gratitude letter writing showed both behavioral increases in gratitude and significantly greater neural modulation by gratitude in the medial prefrontal cortex three months later.[12]

Even better, gratitude seemed to reduce the brain activity in the prefrontal cortex associated with shame, violence, and guilt. Importantly, the prefrontal area of the brain is what presets action, so it would appear that practicing gratitude makes us more likely to be intentional about our actions and less likely act in connection with violence, guilt, or shame. Gratitude also appears to increase intrinsic motivation and awareness of the present[13] while increasing levels of oxytocin, that trust-bonding chemical in the brain, as well.[14]

We cannot say at this point that we understand all the neural-behavioral effects of affirmation and gratitude, but we certainly have enough information to know that they both potentiate healthy brain function within and between individuals both short and long term. They also appear to connect us to a future focus on action and change. Not a bad place to start an epidemic.

In terms of growth mindset, it's important to create interaction that affirms actions, behaviors, and particularly efforts. Praising people for intrinsic beauty, brilliance, or superiority can actually freeze them into a fixed frame. Brandon, back at the horse corral, always praised effort more than results, an important thing to remember in our results-based world. Affirm the attempt, effort, and insight, and you can never go wrong.

Considering the effects of affirmation and appreciation, their link to forward-looking brain centers, and their connection to the brain's formation of intention, A = affirmation/appreciation sets a powerful foundation for any interaction. Sometimes results-oriented individuals will ask whether this isn't just a little too juice-box-for-everyone, snowflakes-need-to-toughen-up fluffery when we all have real problems to solve. The research shows that the connections to effort and results are real. Beyond the evidence that it's helpful, creating affirmation and appreciation comes with the caveat that it has to be sincere and honest, not pandering or condescending. Further, when we are affirming or appreciative with ourselves and others, we're opening a door to what we are about to do, not wrapping a "done perfectly" bow on what we haven't tried yet. The "A" words potentiate uptake and spread of your positive pathogen.

C = Curiosity

We physicians have a unique relationship with curiosity and criticism, inquiry and inquisition. On one hand, the basis of science is to seek understanding, not confirmation of bias or myth. In this sense, curiosity is essential for understanding how the body works, how to design experimental trials, and how to absorb a patient's story. Inquiry helps us learn our skills, expand our knowledge, and understand patients. On the other hand, we are taught to be skeptics who require proof, and we are taught to fix problems, ferret out disease, seek what's *wrong*. No one comes to the emergency department in the middle of the night to hear how wonderfully things are going.

Staying in a posture of curiosity and inquiry can be difficult in a VUCA world, with all the stimuli rushing us and the pressures of performing and responding, to say nothing of the neural hits to our SCARF. Designing interaction around curiosity is powerful, though, particularly in luring our brains out of that rushed and stressed state. Research shows that satisfying our curiosity triggers our reward centers and anchors to the emotional connection to memory in a region of our brain called the hippocampus.[15] Asking questions is a great way to trigger curiosity in the asker and the responder, but our neural state is key. Ask interrogative questions, and you will get a defensive answer; ask curious questions, and you will wake the brain up with intention and creativity.

In essence, curiosity is like a treasure hunt for the brain, and when its questions are answered, the brain is rewarded, happy, and remembers. This is one reason why insight is so valuable—when the brain arrives at its own conclusions, it remembers them and is more likely to act on it.[16] Two plus two is always four, but if you figure it out yourself, you are less likely to forget. It turns out it's not just what we know or hear that drives memory, but how we get there. As we will see, what we ultimately hold powerfully as belief rests on our own exploration to insight and the social cues that support and reinforce that search.

E = Empathy

Empathy is kind of a hot word these days, espoused by many and criticized by some. Depending on which sources you read, *sympathy* is feeling the same feelings someone has and *empathy* is understanding those feeling without sharing them.[17] An article in *Psychology Today* notes that empathy training actually made participants feel *worse* and failed to light up the brain's future intention and reward centers, while compassion training did. In short, empathy made the participants feel pain themselves with no recourse for action.[18]

In his book *Against Empathy,* Paul Bloom argues that emotional empathy alone is incomplete without cognitive consideration that guides compassion, which is traditionally tied to an intent to act.

Although the debate will continue as the research evolves, it would appear that a significant differentiator lies in whether we see the situation of another human as if it were happening to *us* or whether we are trying to be aware of what is happening to *them.*[19] Awareness and attention to what might be occurring to and within *them* triggers our brains in healthier ways than focusing on how it might feel to *us.* Some people refer to this distinction as cognitive empathy vs. emotional empathy.

For our purposes, we will consider empathy as "the capacity to consider the thoughts, perspective, feelings, and background of another by listening to their experience." I like to think of empathy defined this way as a tiny piece of situational awareness. In complex environments, none of us can see the entire system. We piece together "system seeing" by merging overlapping and distinct perspectives, which we can then share as understanding and awareness.

Such empathy implies neither that you perceive another perspective as your own, cognitively or emotionally, nor that you have to agree or disagree with it. Performed well, empathy allows us to acknowledge other perspectives and observations without triggering our own threat response.

Empathy is sensing, and to create sentient approaches to PLV, we need sensing. The biological world is loaded with receptors whose job is to sense and send that sensing on. Our eyes don't blink without sensing, our heart rates don't go up or down without sensing, seeds don't germinate without sensing, and leaders and teams can't create PLV without sensing. Empathy helps us sense.

Create Past-Future Reflection-Action Loops

The entire biological world is filled with feedback. Although we like to think about data, living things run on feedback loops, which shape PLV long before data can be gathered, recorded, tabulated, and formatted, let alone shared, filed in a development plan, and signed off. Right now, as you read these words, uncountable feedback loops keep you breathing, prevent you from breathing too rapidly, slow your heart rate, modulate the muscular tone in thousands of miles of blood vessels, and more.

We humans struggle with feedback because it hits our SCARF buttons (status, certainty, autonomy, relatedness, fairness). As much as we need dense feedback to continually adapt our personal and collective PLV, we struggle both to send and to receive feedback in our conversations.

The excellent article *The Feedback Fallacy* reveals three assumptions embedded in conventional feedback approaches. One, you can't see yourself so someone else should see it for you; two, you are empty of essential extrinsic knowledge and need filling; and three, what you need to be can be objectively described, prescribed, and measured as performance. The data shows that humans are notoriously poor raters of others (but we think we are good at it!).[20]

Worse, stressful environments drive negativity bias, the tendency for us to hear what is negative.[21] We are certainly stressed these days. Recent research suggests that burnout—the syndrome of exhaustion, cynicism, and inefficiency—increased dramatically during the pandemic. Further, according to the authors, burnout seems rooted in causes eerily similar to systemic versions of David Rock's SCARF:[22]

1. Unsustainable workload
2. Perceived lack of control
3. Insufficient rewards for effort
4. Lack of a supportive community
5. Lack of fairness
6. Mismatched values and skills

We find ourselves, then, in systemic environments where feedback is essential, often poorly given, sparse, and likely to be stressful. Ideally, feedback should support an ACE approach to interaction design as a path to PLV. We do know that reinforcement of new behaviors works better ("make the future easier, the past harder") than repeated criticism of old ones,[23] and we also know that insight about what *doesn't* work *is* helpful in creating improved performance.[24]

How, then, can we create feedback loops, similar to the body's, which are abundant, actionable, and effective? How can we design feedback into "flow state" interactions that create insight without expecting individuals to solve a systemic issue like burnout or choose between creating more distress or living in feedback-sparse environments?

In "The Power of Feedback," Hattie and Timperley offer a model focused less on "How good/effective/valid are you?" and instead on the three essential questions feedback must help us answer: "Where are we going, how are we going, and what next?"[25] These feedback questions are remarkably similar to the dynamics governing biological feedback loops, which might be defined by "What do we need, how are we going, and what next?" Notice that the question "How good are you?" is not part of either question sequence, because that question is not relevant to improvement or adaptation.

Designing interactions with the chance to create these questions, repeated iteratively by individuals and groups, moves feedback into the realm of self-reflection at the individual and group level, shifts our state from criticism and inquisition to curiosity and inquiry, and links those reward centers in the brain with forward attention and future action. Such interactions enable us to invite and ask for feedback internally and from others, which has been shown to be beneficial.[26] Such an approach is more likely to benefit from and contribute to neural flow states between participants. Feedback happens abundantly, and is created and invited by all.

Short-Simple-Small (S3)

For an epidemic to happen, both the slow-it-down reflection of infection and pass-it-on action of contagion have to happen multiple times, within and between the same people as well as new people. If something is going to happen, it's going to have to overcome our SCARF resistance, and if it's going to happen multiple times, it had better be brief, simple to do, and involve small get-togethers, which are always easier to wrangle than once-a-year staff meetings.

In light of Aly Mirza's observation that "The first conversation is always the hardest, right?" short, small, and simple all work. In a busy meeting, creating a short interaction broken into small numbers of people with simple instructions can be both effective and frequent without disrupting necessary formal processes. For example, a 60-minute meeting with

20 people has plenty of room for two minutes when 10 pairs of people ask each other the question, "What are you most curious about with regard to our agenda today?" Short means don't take much time; simple means one or two clear things to do; small means put people into small groups.

Go Novel

Some dimensions of effective interaction can seem counterintuitive or "unprofessional" (as opposed to those that are actually unprofessional, like screaming and bullying, which is tolerated all too often although we all circle the multiple-choice answer on the test that says it's not). One of the nice things about focusing on interactions is the energy that grows in the room. Stand at the end of a long table and ask for comments, and you may get some, but you won't get energy, and you won't hear the quieter voices or the wisest thinking. Music and laughter have a host of effects on potentiating learning, increasing dopamine, decreasing cortisol, and decreasing anxiety.[27]

Meditation or even deep breathing can help set the brains in the room for optimum thinking and action. One of our directors at Memorial was a martial artist, and he taught us all how to do deep breathing as a one-minute entry to meetings. There were plenty of eye rolls at first, but I knew it was catching on when I would drop by to visit various units, and they would tell me how helpful it was to breathe for a minute before they tackled their work. "It's unbelievable what that does for our concentration!" one said.

The following list includes points of emphasis as you design interactions. Keep these underlying principles for infectious and contagious interaction in mind as you prototype, practice, and improvise your interactions:

- Design by ACE principles (affirmation/appreciation, curiosity, empathy).
- Design by S3 principles (short, simple, small).

- Create action and reflection loops (What will we do? How will we know?).
- Embrace novel and unique ways of interacting.
- Equalize time speaking and listening for all participants (e.g., "Speak for one minute; listen for one minute.").
- Do not weaponize ("I'm curious why you're such an idiot!").
- Create questions, not commands; invite dialogue, not diatribe.
- Remember "MAP" (mastery/improvement, autonomy/volition, purpose/connection)!
- Improvise from a couple of go-to interaction designs rather than a million potential ones.
- Emphasize what people notice and hear rather than what they proclaim and assume.

From Principles to Patterns

By early 2009, we had anchored the Trust Cycle as a pathogen that could infect our positive future, and we had our list of old and new rules. We were working with the Center for Creative Leadership on an approach to whole-system change, and they brought a lot of expertise in executive development, coaching, and mental models of leadership tailored to the complexity and pace of our place. My "system coach" and later close friend and colleague Laura Quinn, PhD, and I were talking one day about how to hasten our transformation.

"Things aren't moving fast enough," I said.

"These things do take time, though," she said. "You can't rush them."

"I know this Trust Cycle thing has legs," I said. "It's from and of people, not onto them. And the old rules, new rules thing. Also from this place, not dropped in."

"It's not like it isn't working," she thought for a minute. "It's more that people don't have it woven into all the little things they do. It's still a 'thing,' not an everywhere-*way*."

"So how do we get it everywhere?"

"I think it has to be as easy and often as opening a door for someone. You know how two people approach a door—what happens?"

"One person opens the door for the other." I shrugged.

"How often does a fight break out? How often does one person hockey check the other out of the way?"

"Not very often," I laughed.

"That's what we need. Little things that change how people think and act without it taking extra time, because they don't have extra time." We had a pathogen—the Trust Cycle—and we had lots of spaces and containers, but we didn't have interaction rules.

"Okay, I like it . . . but how?"

"Well, you've got all these containers where the Trust Cycle is *known*, but it's not *done*, right?"

"So why isn't it happening?"

"Things are blocking it, I think. Old patterns, old mindsets, busyness. Inertia. I don't think you can proclaim your way out of inertia."

"Hmmm. So what are you thinking?"

"I don't know yet, in any definite way. I just think that we have to flip some of the things people say and do with an alternative habit that changes their reality."

"What do you mean?"

"Look at your old rules. Name two or three of them."

"Okay . . . 'Don't Ask Questions,' 'The King Says,' and 'Nothing About Me Without Me.'"

"Okay, perfect. Those things are in people's heads all the time, right? They need a different experience for those old rules to become the new rules you've all come up with."

Out of that conversation was born our first list of interaction rules candidates. I say candidates because they're really not rules unless people do them, use them, practice them. If they are of no use to people, they're just a flavor-of-the-month flash in the pan. We came up with "Inquiry over Inquisition," "Do you feel heard?" and "Who else needs to know?" These seemed to be good places to start because the "old rules" they replaced were having observable effects in the organization. (Looking back, "Inquiry over Inquisition" is a motto, not an interaction.) People interpreted questions as attacks or "gotcha" cross examinations, they weren't comfortable speaking to formal power, and we were continually forgetting to include relevant stakeholders early and by invitation, so our meetings were always overfull and overscheduled with people keeping an eye out for what they needed to know. Trust was foundering.

We soon found out that starting conversation with "I'm curious . . ." and leading into a question starting with what, how, where, or when created more forthcoming responses. "Do you feel heard?" morphed very quickly into "What is it you need me/us to hear that's important to you?" That phraseology gave people room to articulate their perspective and the "to you" part seemed to invite them personally. People loved "Who else needs to know?" because it solved an immediate need and problem.

We encouraged people to test these out, modify them, and let us know what worked and what didn't. Not surprisingly, some of them were nearly universal, while other interaction rules popped up and were locally useful but did not catch on everywhere. They were used where they worked. They all helped us create the common ground, dialogue skill, collective intelligence, and trust as colleagues that we need to shape the positive future.

You can create as many interaction rules as there are combinations of people who bump into each other. Following is a sample of interaction rules that fit the S3 principle and have helped people create PLV.

Affirmation

- What positive things are we seeing?
- What should we celebrate and high-five?
- Here's one thing I really appreciate about what I heard from you/see you doing . . .

Curiosity

- I want to point out something I appreciate about what you are doing/how you are thinking.
- What is one thing you are grateful for/curious about?
- I am curious about what/how/why . . .

Empathy

- What is one thing you see that perhaps I/we may not?
- I want to be sure I'm/we're thinking of this from an angle beyond my/our own. Help me/us understand how you are seeing things.
- What is the most important thing for you in the work we are about to do?
- What is it you'd like me to understand?
- What is most important here to you?

Reflection-Action Loops

- Start every meeting or huddle with one minute of quiet silence.
- How will we know when we are we done working/talking today?
- What do you need from me/us? (Here's what I/we need from you.)
- Who else needs to know what we're thinking or doing, and when?
- "Fist to five" (everyone raises a hand with a fist or from one to five fingers as an answer): How much (candor, honesty, curiosity, discipline, listening, etc.) are we showing right now?
- Tell me one thing you don't think we're paying enough attention to yet.
- How have we gotten a little better just now?
- How do we know?
- What are we learning?
- What next, who next, how next?
- What's one way we're getting in each other's way? What might we try differently?
- When will we next check in?

- What went differently than I/you thought it would? What surprised you/us?
- What did I/you notice that I/you didn't expect?
- Do you feel heard?/What do you need me to hear?
- What's one thing we did today that's different and better than what we would have done previously?
- How can we spread and multiply what just happened?
- What's one small thing we can do to improve how we work/think right now?
- What's one small thing we can do to make our work easier and better right now?

The Four Magic Questions

- What's happening right now? (at the level of PLV, execution, communication, etc.—pick your area of focus)
- How do we know?
- What are we learning?
- What will we do next to adapt the way we intend?

In Masese, Uganda, the teachers and staff would need to create their new interaction rules as well. They were accustomed to instructing and directing children, consistent with what they had been taught and their belief that children needed to be told, not asked. Their recognition of creativity as "something from nothing" helped them appreciate the need for the children to find their own way at times. Accordingly, they simply agreed to ask as often as possible, "What could we do here to be creative?" It was simple, short, and an effective invitation to each other and to the children, and the barrier to asking that question was very low. They just had to build a secondary reflection loop, asking themselves as a staff, "What happens when we ask that question? What are we seeing and noticing?"

The creativity, manifested in interaction patterns, flowed out of the classroom and into the common area. Where once there was packed dirt, the school has a garden that feeds fresh vegetables to the children twice a week, a rare dietary upgrade in a place where fresh vegetables are more than what many of the students' families can afford. The leader of the HELP organization at the school, Ronnie Sitanga, says that the biggest change in his internal interactions with himself was to ask himself how a problem was a chance to create a new solution rather than an obstacle he had to remove. When the pandemic hit and most schools closed, he asked the staff the simple question, "How can we be creative with solutions?" While other schools simply closed, HELP school created a mobile teaching force, and the teachers met the students in small bubbles in or near their homes. The school has been so successful planting fruit trees, each "owned" by two or three students who tend them, that at the time of this writing, the school is getting ready to teach other schools how to engage children in growing trees in their schools. The organization that supplied the trees, accustomed to poor aftercare and tree death, has committed to give them one thousand more fruit trees. If trees and creativity have become an epidemic, the company is now sourcing contagion via HELP school in recognition of their promise as a successful "idea exporter" of tree planting. The HELP school has become an infectious and contagious node of agroforestry in a deforested country.

How Leaders Build Interaction Rules

As infection moves from small to big, so does transformation. Designing interaction follows a path from "I" to "We" to "They" (although we often prefer to organize transformation less effectively from "They" to "We" to "I"!). Leaders can begin observing the effect of particular interaction designs on themselves and others simply by practicing a few and asking people what they noticed and whether they are trying or would try some of these approaches. I often have found it interesting to hear people notice and appreciate an interaction design's impact on themselves—and then find out that while they're happy to benefit from a particular interaction, they themselves aren't spreading it! I've created my own little rule around that one: "What did you like about how we interacted here?" and then, "I look forward to hearing what you notice and hear when you try it with your people." I often have to ask four or five times before they move from appreciating it to *doing* it in a new environment. That pattern is normal and shows the value of inquiry-based repetition in supporting the shift from insight to action and from occasional attempt to habitual action.

As essential as it is for leaders to model by example, the interactions grounded in ACE, reflection-action loops, and S3 (short, simple, small), staking your epidemic on your own skill and visibility as a personal role model is both insufficient and inefficient. You can't be more than your "one," and you can't be *in* every interaction, but you do get to decide how you want to design interactions. "Model" has another meaning beyond "be a singular example": to "design a prototype."[28] If you can convene people around relational patterns that truly create PLV in micro whenever they practice them and ones that are easily adopted and easily conveyed, you can magnify effect beyond your "blast radius." If you can shift patterns of interactions so that they are always constructive, that pattern will amplify as long as you and others tend to it and create positive social reinforcement.

Observation of the interaction patterns in your environment, and inviting others into that observation, is a key step. You can actually design effective interaction simply inviting people to ask each other, in pairs, at the end of an event, "What did you notice that helped us work? Where did we get in each other's way a bit?" Splitting people into pairs and then combining those pairs into four and asking them to look for trends is a great way for everyone's voice to get in the mix while minimizing the negative social pressure of speaking into a whole room. You can then sift the trends and ask, "What next?"

As people begin to create interaction rules, they often designate "interaction" that is more "motto" than practice, as I did with Inquiry over Inquisition. For example, they may say, "Be respectful," or "Always listen." What they are after is fantastic and effective, but they have not yet designed an *interaction* as much as they have asserted a value. "Be respectful," might be designed as an interaction if people agreed to give everyone in a group 30 seconds to articulate to two conversation partners what is most important to them in the work they are about to do, and give each of those triplets 30 seconds to share their distilled priorities with the larger group. Those priorities can then be observed, tracked, and reflected upon ("Did we do this? Did we find it helpful?"). For listening, a group might decide to say, "I really want to listen carefully to what you say, so when you're done, I'm going to wait five seconds to reflect before I respond," or "When I listen to people, I commit to shut my phone off."

The number of interaction rules is limitless. Observing your environments, and inviting those in them to observe their own thought and action patterns, is an essential part of inviting people to design their interaction patterns to increase PLV. Alternatively, you can always make a suggestion. As you think about how to design interaction rules that serve what people know they need ("We all talk too much!" or "We are too quick to list reasons why not!") and especially the needs they may *not* be aware of yet, you can even model a rule to open the door to optimal interaction patterns: simply ask people what they need from the work at hand. What do they need from each other? Like any good interaction rule, this one scales well across topics and levels. People can ask each other at the beginning and end of conversations and tasks, "What do you need from me/us?" and declare, "Here's what I/we need from you." I read recently about the reality that we often don't know when a conversation is over[29] and that invariably one participant stops too soon or goes on too long. People could create a rule for that before, during, and after a conversation if they wanted: "Let's check in to know when we're done talking." The nice thing about interaction rules is that you can make them up, test and try them, tweak them, add them, or discard them, simply by asking, "How did this help us? Would continuing this rule help us more, or are we no longer needing it?" Keep observing, trying, and sifting, and the right patterns for your group will float to the top of your work.

Years ago at Memorial we started a house-wide safety huddle to improve our safety for patients. We designed the container of the huddle to be open to anyone, 15 minutes long, and grounded in several key questions: "What are we grateful for? What did we notice that was or could cause risk to patients or staff? What do we need to do to eliminate this risk in 24 hours?"

The results were impressive—a threefold reduction in our serious safety event rate in six months, but so was the energy and the learning and speed. We weren't accustomed to changing *anything* in 24 hours.

That huddle is still going on today, over a decade later and long after its founding executives have left. What I took out of it in terms of framing interaction were what I call the "four magic questions": *What's happening here* (that we notice and appreciate)? *How do we know (*interrogates bias*)*? *What are we learning* ("I'm curious . . .")? *What might we do next (action loop)*? These four questions can incorporate the principles of ACE, reflection-action, and S3 (simple, short, small) and can be asked by one person or a hundred, every hour or every day. They are only one example of an interaction rule, but they illustrate how such interaction can simultaneously integrate the principles in this chapter and movement toward PLV at all levels.

Interaction patterns invite participants to express the effect of a pathogen uniquely *and* uniformly, much the way a disease has certain common symptoms but every person has a slightly different set of symptoms unique to that person. In this sense, being a host-human in a social epidemic becomes not just a participatory process but an intentional one, a key to leverage the power of individual volition and the supportive tailwind of social pressure. For the purposes of leading epidemically, think of the term "host" as a one who welcomes and convenes the conversion from idea to action. All sorts of behavioral habits can pass from person to person without their thinking about it, but if your goal as a leader is the richest texture of PLV scaled, you will want to cultivate widespread intention and participation. The people in your epidemic are not objects; they are authors, creators, and participants as well as listeners, watchers, and receivers. For this both-and dynamic to flourish at any given interaction, let alone as patterns in your larger positive epidemic, it must originate and flourish at the most micro level.

Notes

1. S. Fisher Qua and Keith McCandless, "More Magic, Less Mystery," *Medium*, May 16, 2020, `https://medium.com/@keithmccandless/more-magic-less-mystery-f6e03d19f9bb`.
2. Nicholas A. Christakis and James H. Fowler, *Connected* (New York: Little, Brown Spark, 2009), 22.
3. Judith E. Glaser, *Conversational Intelligence: How Great Leaders Build Trust and Get Extraordinary Results* (New York: Bibliomotion, 2014), 61.
4. Brian T. Pentland and Martha S. Feldman, "Organizational Routines as a Unit of Analysis," *Industrial and Corporate Change* 14, no. 5 (August 26, 2005): 796, `https://doi.org/10.1093/icc/dth070`.
5. Naomi I. Eisenberger, Matthew D. Lieberman, and Kipling D. Williams, "Does Rejection Hurt? An FMRI Study of Social Exclusion," *Science* 302, no. 5643 (October 10, 2003): 290–292, `https://doi.org/10.1126/science.1089134`.
6. Stephen Ray Flora, "Praise's Magic Reinforcement Ratio: Five to One Gets the Job Done," *The Behavior Analyst Today*, September 22, 2000, `https://www.thefreelibrary.com/Praise%27s+magic+reinforcement+ratio%3a+five+to+one+gets+the+job+done.-a0170112823`.
7. "Hearing Positive Verbs Can Induce Unconscious Physical Response," *ScienceDaily*, December 5, 2012, `https://www.sciencedaily.com/releases/2012/12/121205200055.htm`.
8. Janine M. Dutcher et al., "Neural Mechanisms of Self-affirmation's Stress Buffering Effects," *Social Cognitive and Affective Neuroscience* 15, no. 10 (October 2020): 1086, `https://doi.org/10.1093/scan/nsaa042`.
9. Christopher N. Cascio et al., "Self-Affirmation Activates Brain Systems Associated with Self-Related Processing and Reward and Is Reinforced by

Future Orientation," *Social Cognitive and Affective Neuroscience* 11, no. 4 (April 2016): 621, https://doi.org/10.1093/scan/nsv136.

10. Assad Zahid, Jonathan Hong, and Christopher J. Young, "Surgical Supervisor Feedback Affects Performance: A Blinded Randomized Study," *Cureus* 9, no. 5 (May 25, 2017), https://dx.doi.org/10.7759%2Fcureus.1276.
11. Glenn R. Fox et al., "Neural Correlates of Gratitude," *Frontiers in Psychology* 6 (September 30, 2015): https://dx.doi.org/10.3389%2Ffpsyg.2015.01491.
12. Prathik Kini et al., "The Effects of Gratitude Expression on Neural Activity," *NeuroImage* 128 (March 2016): 1, https://doi.org/10.1016/j.neuroimage.2015.12.040.
13. Madhuleena Roy Chowdhury, "The Neuroscience of Gratitude and How It Affects Anxiety and Grief," PositivePsychology.com, accessed January 7, 2021, https://positivepsychology.com/neuroscience-of-gratitude/.
14. Sara B. Algoe and Baldwin M. Way, "Evidence for a Role of the Oxytocin System, Indexed by Genetic Variation in CD38, in the Social Bonding Effects of Expressed Gratitude," *Social Cognitive and Affective Neuroscience* 9, no. 12 (December 2014): 1855, https://doi.org/10.1093/scan/nst182.
15. Marieke Jepma et al., "Neural Mechanisms Underlying the Induction and Relief of Perceptual Curiosity," *Frontiers in Behavioral Neuroscience* 6 (February 13, 2012): https://doi.org/10.3389/fnbeh.2012.00005; Matthias J. Gruber, Bernard D. Gelman, and Charan Ranganath, "State of Curiosity Modulate Hippocampus-Dependent Learning via the Dopaminergic Circuit," *Neuron* 84, no. 2 (October 22, 2014): 486, https://doi.org/10.1016/j.neuron.2014.08.060.
16. David Rock and Jeffrey Schwartz, "The Neuroscience of Leadership," *Strategy+Business* Summer 2006, no. 43 (May 30, 2006): https://www.strategy-business.com/article/06207.
17. "What's the Difference Between 'Sympathy' and 'Empathy'?" Merriam-Webster.com Dictionary, accessed February 10, 2021, https://www.merriam-webster.com/words-at-play/sympathy-empathy-difference.

18. Tara Well, "Compassion Is Better Than Empathy," *Psychology Today*, March 4, 2017, https://www.psychologytoday.com/us/blog/the-clarity/201703/compassion-is-better-empathy.
19. Claus Lamm, C. Daniel Batson, and Jean Decety, "The Neural Substrate of Human Empathy: Effects of Perspective-Taking and Cognitive Appraisal," *Journal of Cognitive Neuroscience* 19, no. 1 (January 2007): 42, https://doi.org/10.1162/jocn.2007.19.1.42.
20. Marcus Buckingham and Ashley Goodall, "The Feedback Fallacy," *Harvard Business Review*, March–April 2019, https://hbr.org/2019/03/the-feedback-fallacy.
21. Therese Huston, "Giving Critical Feedback Is Even Harder Remotely," *Harvard Business Review*, January 26, 2021, https://hbr.org/2021/01/giving-critical-feedback-is-even-harder-remotely.
22. Jennifer Moss, "Beyond Burned Out," *Harvard Business Review*, February 10, 2021, https://hbr.org/2021/02/beyond-burned-out.
23. Paula Alsher, "Your Reinforcement Strategy: A Powerful Change Management Tool for Getting Better, Faster Project Results," Implementation Management Associates, posted March 16, 2017, https://www.imaworldwide.com/blog/your-reinforcement-strategy-a-powerful-change-management-tool-for-getting-better-faster-project-results; Jenifer Marshall Lippincott, "Our Brains Are to Blame: The Neuroscience of Feedback," Training Industry, February 9, 2018, https://trainingindustry.com/articles/performance-management/our-brains-are-to-blame-the-neuroscience-of-feedback/.
24. Assad Zahid, Jonathan Hong, and Christopher J. Young, "Surgical Supervisor Feedback Affects Performance: A Blinded Randomized Study," *Cureus* 9, no. 5 (May 25, 2017): https://dx.doi.org/10.7759%2Fcureus.1276.
25. John Hattie and Helen Timperley, "The Power of Feedback," *Review of Educational Research* 77, no. 1 (March 1, 2007): 86, http://www.columbia.edu/~mvp19/ETF/Feedback.pdf.
26. David Rock, Beth Jones, and Chris Weller, "Using Neuroscience to Make Feedback Work and Feel Better," *Strategy+Business* Winter 2018, no. 93 (August 27, 2018): https://www.strategy-business.com/article/Using-Neuroscience-to-Make-Feedback-Work-and-Feel-Better.

27. Brandon M. Savage et al., "Humor, Laughing, Learning, and Health! A Brief Review," *Advances in Physiology Education* 41, no. 3 (July 5, 2017), https://doi.org/10.1152/advan.00030.2017.
28. "Model," Merriam-Webster.com Dictionary, accessed January 20, 2020, https://www.merriam-webster.com/dictionary/model.
29. Adam M. Mastroianni et al., "Do Conversations End When People Want Them To?" PNAS 118, no. 10 (March 9, 2021), https://doi.org/10.1073/pnas.2011809118.

8 Multipliers

An important function of almost every system is to ensure its own perpetuation.

—*Donella H. Meadows*

If interaction design takes an epidemic from potential to real, multipliers take the fragile early outbreak of disease from small and stuttering to going and growing. Interactions codify how people collide and connect in the brine of pathogen and supportive conditions, but epidemics require multipliers to demonstrate both rapid growth and stable presence. Without multipliers, leaders cannot scale a positive pathogen into the new patterns of thought, action, and interaction necessary for PLV within their organizations. In Masese, the teachers and students are growing creativity and trees, and in the Spring of 2021 they began infecting other schools with these pathogens, but they need more multipliers. They are in a country that, once widely forested, now has only 8 percent forest cover and continues to lose trees.

The Value of Many

We all know examples of positive ideas and practices within teams or companies that do not blossom into widely practiced patterns. They are lurking unrecognized or underappreciated where you are right now.

Those healthier patterns, and the people that embody them, will linger in your human system somewhere, smoldering and invisible, and may even grow slowly over time, but they are unlikely to show explosive growth or wide, stable diffusion. Those patterns are also at risk of disappearing. It's why athletes change teams and why people leave jobs—the people that leave are the ones who have the power to do so, and they leave because they do not see the patterns they need to see. Companies that can't add and create positive patterns while they discard and marginalize negative ones are at risk. Their internal ecosystems initially grow stale and rigid, and then later collapse.

The dynamics of self-organization suggest that if you just sit and watch and wait, *something* will self-organize. Unfortunately, you won't know what that will be or when that will happen. It happened to the British Empire in the eighteenth century by way of the Boston Tea Party, and it happens every time you get influenza or a cold. As leaders, we do not lead by waiting for accidents and random events, though. For leaders, multipliers add the speed and focus necessary to lead intentionally with self-organization, adjacent to our more mechanistic techniques. For most of us, the idea of speed is associated with increased effort and a sense of *pushing*. In epidemics, speed arises from the number and density of interactions—the secret sauce that takes the successful prototypes of infection and disease and floods a whole population. If you have put the time in to shape ideas as pathogens, set generative conditions, and design interactions that shift how people think and act, multipliers are the fun part. Multipliers are the wand you wave as you bring the participants of your—and *their*—epidemic into symphonic synergy.

When epidemics go from bubbling to booming, it is because of multipliers. Imagine two people locked in a room, one infected with a powerful pathogen that causes curiosity and the other uninfected. The interaction design between the two people creates transmission of disease, contagion, but it's the ability for infected persons to infect increasingly large numbers of people that multiplies the effect of initial transmission. Those two people may be very contagious to each other, for example, in terms of passing the curiosity disease, but if it's only the two of them locked in a room until after the curiosity disease has run its course, their mini-epidemic dies for lack of a multiplier.

The R value, or reproductive number, we heard so much about during the COVID pandemic articulates the multiplier phenomenon. It refers to how many people a given disease case infects via contagion. If an epidemic's R number is three, each diseased person creates three more additional cases. For our two people locked in a room with a 10-day disease of Overwhelming Curiosity, their R number is only 0.5 (the first person's is 1, as that person creates one additional infection; the second person's R number is 0, as that person can't pass it on because the door is closed, so their total cases are two, with total new cases of 1; total cases created divided by the number of people with disease $= \frac{1+0}{2} = 0.5$. For epidemics to grow, they must have an R value higher than one; each case must create *more* than one other case. The higher the R, the faster the epidemic will grow.

As we see in our example of two people with Overwhelming Curiosity disease, driving a higher R number—multiplying—can be as simple as opening that locked room and letting people stream in and letting our two diseased people walk out and begin interacting with others. In one sense, multiplying your epidemic is that easy: just take down the barriers that keep people from interacting with each other.

When we look at the COVID pandemic, however, we realize that a couple of key interaction dimensions were in play that may not be in play where you lead. First, people were bumping into each other in sufficiently varied ways that the virus, once it was out of its "little room" where it started (always the easiest way to stop an epidemic, and a point not lost on oppressive regimes and leaders of any stripe), could move relatively unimpeded. If COVID ran into one household that didn't have contact with anyone else, it ended up in a version of our locked room and died, even if everyone in the house fell ill. In the real world, there were so many combinations of human-to-human contact, however, so many planes, stores, gymnasiums, churches, restaurants, grocery stores, and subways, that the door, somewhere, was always open. Such redundant interfacing may not be present where you are leading until you design it.

As you think about it, though, there must be plenty of casual interfaces in your organization. People bump into each other in the cafeteria, in the parking lot, on the way in and out of offices, elevators, warehouses, and shop floors. Isn't that why we social distanced? Even under the conditions of social distancing, people are interfacing via video calls, Facebook, LinkedIn, and Instagram. If we could catch COVID bumping into each other, why can't we catch and spread innovation, high reliability, and critical thinking skills in the same way?

Different Kinds of Social Pathogens

The reason that the casual interfaces between people can effectively cause a disease like COVID but not one like innovation or collaboration is that COVID is a *simple* pathogen, while the kind of things leaders help spread in order to grow and sustain PLV are *complex* pathogens. This doesn't mean that SARS-CoV-2's biology is simple or primitive; simple and complex refer to ease of transmission. Damon Centola, in his book *How Behavior Spreads: The Science of Complex Contagions*, differentiates what he calls contagions as simple or complex. Simple contagions are things like game scores, weather reports, or release dates for new phones or music. Once someone encounters a simple contagion, it's easy to yell it out in a crowded room or text it to 40 people, any or all of whom can just as easily move it on. If people didn't catch the game score or the new Taylor Swift single drop date, repeating the information will get the job done if they were in the other room at the time of the first announcement or if their phone battery had just died. Neither effort nor any lowering of resistance is required for these simple things to diffuse through populations.[1]

Complex contagions, or pathogens in our epidemic construct, require people to change their patterns of thought and behavior. Simply repeating the same information over and over can have some effect, which is how rumors become "true," a reality often used by politicians and agitators, but changing behaviors and belief systems takes more than multiple thoughtless repetitions. As Centola points out, "while multiple exposures to the same infected individual may be sufficient for simple contagions to spread, multiple *sources* [italics mine] of exposure are needed to diffuse complex contagions." Complex pathogens require multiplying the number of interactions *and* the number of distinct and influential human contacts.

The patterns of communication and information flow in a team and an organization may be sufficiently redundant and diverse within a team, organization, or community to traffic simple pathogens like game scores and weather reports. Org charts, committees, and protocols may enable a high R value for simple pathogens like instructions or commands, but they don't enable a high R value for complex pathogens unless you build multipliers for complex pathogens. Unfortunately, complex pathogens, the ones that change patterns of thought and action, encounter opposing patterns of embedded resistance in your organization that are neither random nor likely to just wilt away.

Resistance Is Everywhere

Those resistance patterns have three forms: neural, structural, and social. Neural resistance is our biologically designed capacity to go to threat state, to continue what is automatic and easy, and to look out at the world with bias, that perspective we have on the universe and any and all topics within it as correct because *we think it is so*. Structural resistance is anything that keeps us from being in the same space where we can bump into each other. People working in operating rooms are less likely to bump into people working in the hospital cafeteria, and people working in revenue cycle are unlikely to run into people working in marketing. Social resistance derives from the gravitational power of people who comprise our social context and support our biases, opinions, worldviews, and perspectives. All three of these kinds of resistance lurk in and around individuals, teams, and networks.

Thoughtful interaction design can and must address these forms of resistance within individuals and populations, but interaction design alone cannot overwhelm the stable array of neural, structural, and social resistance until and unless you leverage multiplier strategies in your leadership efforts. You can contract influenza or COVID-19 from anybody: enough coughs and handshakes at the right distance, and you will catch one of them sooner or later. HIV, the virus that causes AIDS, is more complex. No amount of hand shaking or coughing can transmit it to you. Even when you change the interaction from coughing to sexual contact, influenza and COVID are easier to catch and pass than HIV. It often takes more exposures to get HIV than it does to get the common cold. Complex behavioral pathogens are even more different than that. The interaction design has to move you through an arc from awareness to consideration to insight to intent to attempt to habit (that's the neural part). The multipliers have to be sufficiently repetitive and reinforcing, and social influence, not just repetition, has to be designed outside and around those interactions. As Centola emphasizes, more exposures are sufficient for simple pathogens, but complex pathogens require more sources *and* more exposure. Creating the right kind of neural, structural, and social multipliers will optimize the chance that the new patterns rising in the micro-interactions that work so well will normalize into stable macro patterns that shape a team's or an organization's thoughts and actions.

Building Multipliers

Easy Addition

"Adding more" does work, and it takes advantage of the inherent contagion you have built into your interaction design. As casinos and banks know, if there is a potential benefit to a particular small action, repeating it millions of times will compound the positive probability inherent in the small transaction. For banks, these probabilities are certainties: when there is a fee associated with using an ATM card, increased use of the ATM card creates more and more revenue according to a fixed fee and multiplied by the number of transactions. "Doing more" doesn't require a positive probability of 100 percent to be effective, though. In most casino games, the positive chance of money to the house is far smaller. If it weren't, you would recognize the casino as a reverse bank, taking your money every time you played instead of protecting your money while you paid a small fee. Accordingly, casino games give the casino a *small* chance of winning. Casinos know with mathematical certainty that they will win some and lose some, and while you drink and laugh, they make sure the tiny interactions—slot pulls, dice rolls, blackjack hands—just keep going. The positive advantage confers to them just as certainly as it does to the bank, but less offensively to you than if you just lost every hand or roll. In effect, they deploy the S3 interaction principle (short, simple, small) and design the games so that millions of easy repetition keep you engaged and distracted while they let the winnings pile up. Any given small casino interaction has chance; multiplied together they approach certainty.

If your epidemic is built on interactions that create a positive effect a certain percentage of the time, doing more of them will strengthen the pattern. You can run more interactions per unit meeting, for example. Having people run one rule together at the beginning of the meeting, one during the middle, and one at the end will allow people to solidify three new thinking habits in the space where they were doing only one. You can also create more spaces where the interaction rules are in play. Surprised at the positive response to their invitational pathogen, the Microsoft Growth Groups founders were able to run more "containers" in a larger number of groups, leveraging the positive word of mouth from earlier groups to drive an even larger number for the second cohort.

Just as COVID thrived wherever more people were crammed into confined spaces, you can add people to given spaces. Doing so can quickly change the tenor of an entire meeting or event, but that doesn't mean you can't leverage the value of bringing uninfected individuals into a space where contagion can "catch" them. At Memorial, we began inviting people who we thought had an interest in leadership, as defined by the inviting manager, to our monthly leadership forum. At first, only a couple of people came, but as we kept inviting, and as managers saw their peers doing it, and the people who came had positive experiences, it became second nature for new people to benefit from and add to the work we designed in that container around seeing and listening to future leaders.

We did the same thing at our quality huddle as soon as we realized the same people were coming daily and not communicating back to their floors or creating secondary huddles. Once we started rotating people out of work shifts into the huddle and asking floors (via essentially a new interaction rule) how they were spawning local huddles linked to the main safety huddle, we were able to involve a far larger number of people who were benefiting from and contributing to the way we were thinking, acting, and energizing about quality, and the results showed it.

When you go epidemic into a new space, it's helpful to remember the relative difficulty of the first case; it is far easier for positive disease to hop from person to person than to rise from nothing. When you introduce your pathogen in a new space, introduce it with numbers of people, at least pairs. The Growth Groups founders did this with their growth leads, pairing them up, grouping them together in debriefs and curricular planning, and pulling their new leads from the infected populations of previous growth groups. At HELP school in Masese, the teachers were already infected with the "something-from-nothing creativity" pathogen and carried social authority, so it was relatively easy to seed all the classrooms, especially when the teachers looped back to one another with a collegial inquiry rule to ask one another,

"*What's working? What are we learning? What can we try next to help the students think creatively?*"

Broadcasting and Storytelling

Another way to involve more people is by creating public learning. At Memorial Health System, a particular surgeon and nurse colleague who had been instrumental in leading one of our key programs had negatively impacted their unit for some time because of their difficulty working together. It was one of those things everyone knew and suffered from but no one discussed. Through some work with a coach, which was requested and supported by colleagues and peers in a confidential process, the two reached a higher level of dyad function. It struck them and others that their conflict was not just specific to their personalities but was seminal and archetypal to our organization. The two agreed to share their story openly with a much wider leadership group.

During a wide-ranging interview in front of 250 people, the two of them candidly reflected on their own learning, their vulnerabilities, their insights, and their lessons learned as individuals and as a leadership dyad. That public conversation itself, held in front of dozens of peers and with a question-and-answer format, probably would have had some benefit, but we also tossed in a before-and-after interaction design as well. Before the two started sharing their story, we asked everyone in the room to write down an issue between two people in their area of the organization. We set three criteria: the issue had to be one that was creating wider impact, it wasn't being addressed, and it had been sitting there a while. We split them into pairs and asked them to share their issue and supporting details. Then we let the public interview unfold.

Afterward, we split people into different pairs to reflect on the cost of their own "unaddressed issue" and to develop an approach for dealing with it, even if the first step was simply asking for assistance. What rose out of that common experience of a public story and mini-interviews was that what appeared to be a specific trouble spot was both more universal and specific than people might have originally thought, and that we had a pattern of not dealing with such things. Further, the interviewees brought up a point not lost on people as they created their own plans: they had to face their own vulnerabilities, biases, and egos, and look them in the eye. By the time we were done, everyone had a plan for tackling a tough issue that was stuck, and everyone had public support and positive pressure for doing so.

Storytelling is a particularly powerful form of creating broad exposure, particularly when the storytellers can credibly and humbly speak in the first person not so much about what they know as about what they learned (growth mindset!), and when they can speak as "one of us," rather than "one of them." If these criteria can be met, the chances are high that a large number of people will perceive the elements of the story—patterns of thinking, acting, and interacting—as credible and "like me." Combining such storytelling with the interaction design principles in Chapter 7 before and after the story, which we essentially did with our physician-nurse interview, can be a very positive multiplier, particularly when the practice becomes a norm in itself, not a novel and unusual event. This interaction–interview combination can be leveraged via technology, which we will address in Chapter 10.

In a sense, multiplying is that easy—just keep adding to what you're doing. Small, positive effects of frequent interactions—think casinos—really add up. In particular, tracking small bits of progress, which can be done via the four magic questions in Chapter 7, increases our motivation over longer arcs of progress.[2]

Well-designed interactions repeated with additional people and spaces can counter neural, structural, and social resistance. Even if your approach is not perfectly infectious or contagious, relentless repetition will multiply the impact of any small effect. Neither pathogen, nor conditions, nor interaction, nor multipliers have to be perfect—they just have to happen enough so that the "winning" patterns of thought, action, and interaction keep popping up and being passed along, and the "losers" become mathematically marginal and phase out. Blackjack and Roulette don't work this way, but biology does. If something stays in your system, it's providing a value, even if it's one you don't intend or understand. If it has no value, it will disappear.

The slow spread of change, the entrenchment of mindsets, the intransigence of bad habits and the fragility of new ones in populations remind us that more reps, more people, and more spaces are often insufficient to overcome the resistance in a social system. Remember the growth mindset study in which ninth graders with training sometimes improved and sometimes didn't? For the students to really become infected with growth mindset, they needed peer support for it.[3] Continuing to add people and places may or may not evolve to mass effects. Fortunately, we have more tools in our box to help multiply the effect of interaction rules in a population.

Mix Numbers and Times

One of the things I enjoyed most during my CEO years was welcoming new employees to the organization. Every two weeks I had a chance to meet with them and get their thoughts about why healthcare was important to them and what they hoped to find and intended to create in the organization. I started by asking them to answer two questions out loud and together. The first was a true-false question: "Healthcare is a team sport." True. The second was a sentence completion: "When you want something done right . . ." They all answered correctly as we have been taught, "*Do It Yourself!*" We spent the rest of the time talking about how they could help build an organization where individual commitment and skills counted and where collective intelligence resulted.

By now behavioral scientists have established abundant evidence that a smart team supersedes a smart individual unless the individual houses particular knowledge not in the team. In the delightfully titled *What Makes a Strong Team? Using Collective Intelligence to Predict Team Performance in League of Legends*, a multi-institution team of researchers explored the design of group intelligence in dispersed, fluid, digitally connected teams that are so common today. They note that collective intelligence "is built upon some combination of individual members' attributes and group structures, processes, and norms. In both face-to-face and online groups, CI has been predicted by a high proportion of women in the group, high level of average member social perceptiveness, moderate level of cognitive diversity, large amounts of communication and equal distribution of communication."[4,5,6] Both in and out of the gaming arena, we continue to discover the emergent reality of team intelligence.[7] In "The New Science of Building Great Teams," Alex Pentland from MIT notes several factors that influence how teams perform, regardless of content or topic. Two of them are that "everyone on the team talks and listens the same amount of time as others, and their contributions are relatively short and to the point." The article goes on to note that team "members face each other while engaging in conversations that can be characterized as energetic."[8] The issue of time sharing is further supported in other literature as well, as is the value of mixed gender groups, with the presence of women in particular being attributed to higher levels of social sensitivity, which can be described as "how well group members perceive each others' emotions,"[9] the quality we called "empathy" in Chapter 7. Interestingly, for teams to perform optimally and multiply the intelligence of the individuals that comprise it, not all of the conversation has to be focused on the work tasks at hand. Casual conversation actually counts and actually helps teams work.[10] The act of participating in healthy conversation about *anything* helps groups elevate their level of function.

Aside from factors that define a group's constituents or how they communicated per se, James Surowiecki's 2004 book *The Wisdom of Crowds* lays out four conditions that allow a crowd to be smarter than any one member: diversity of perspective, independent and uninfluenced opinions, decentralized reliance on local knowledge, and aggregation of those observations. For leaders who seek to mitigate the neural, structural, and social inhibitors of uptake and diffusion of new ideas in a population, this growing body of knowledge opens the door to infinite possibilities about how to put the interaction rules designed in Chapter 6 into practice so that they multiply motivation, belief, and results.

Imagine you're in a room with 10 people, and you want to multiply the effect of an interaction rule so that it can more effectively infect each of the individuals in the room and increase the contagion—the ability to receive and pass it—among them. Imagine also that the interaction rule you decide to use is to ask the question, "What is the most important thing we have to pay attention to right now?" to enhance the group's awareness and focus. This question links easily to any number of subsequent interaction rules—*What do we need from each other to create success? When will we loop back to check on progress and insights learned? How can we remain focused and simultaneously open to new ideas and opportunities?*—but for now you are just wanting to get things off to a good start. You want to multiply the impact of this simple interaction within the room, leveraging every perspective to create optimal intelligence.

You could just ask the question, aptly applying the rule yourself, and wait for the answer. What is likely to follow is a pattern we all recognize. After a pause, a couple of people, usually extroverts with strong social positions in the room, will share their perspective. From a facilitative standpoint, you can invite quieter members of the room to share their perspectives as well, and with some effort by you, you can manage to get people's thoughts out, or at least some of them. It will take some time, and while that time is going by people's attention will slip to their phones and other priority tasks. You also will not be able to eliminate the invisible cloak of bias inherent in the rules that govern who speaks and what are acceptable and unacceptable things to say. As a facilitator, you will also be using a lot of your own energy to read the room as you unilaterally try to wrangle the variables that you know optimize collective intelligence.

What predominantly happens in our hypothetical scenario involving you and 9 other people is that while 10 people are in the room, there is usually only one interaction going on per unit time. Whether you're standing or sitting, using a table or not, next to a large window with a soothing view or underground in a windowless bunker, the interaction per unit time in this scenario is sparse. If you think about it, a lot of organizational activity takes place this way. Even if you have the right interaction rule at play in many spaces in your organization or team, it is probably not linked to multipliers that allow multiple people to be thinking, acting, and interacting optimally at any given time. We don't want occasional group intelligence and occasional individual participation—we want both these things to grow exponentially—without cramming more into already exhausting days.

Authors Eric Garton and Michael Mankins emphasize in a 2020 article in *Harvard Business Review* that productive companies effectively leverage human time, talent, and discretional energy to muster productivity.[11] They note that during the pandemic, companies that leverage these variables well are now 40 percent more productive than those that don't. How well we multiply interaction per unit time, without taking people's extra time, which they need to do their work, has become an essential capacity in our era. Teams and companies have to optimize the polarity of individual work and effort and group work and effort, sometimes when we're in the same room, and increasingly when we're not. Individual intelligence has to multiply collective intelligence and vice versa.

Group interactions like the one in our preceding hypothetical scenario are not leveraging those things very well, which is certainly one reason that we are all acculturated to "do it yourself" if we want it done right, a wonderful foundation for personal accountability but a barrier to collective intelligence. How then?

Based on the research on smart teams and collective intelligence, you could take the same rule and multiply its impact by doing the following things: Break people into five one-on-one conversations, each three minutes long, each made up of two 90-second halves. Each person talks during one half while the other listens, and then the pair switches speaking-listening roles. After nine minutes, you will have multiplied the interaction rule from one (you speaking or listening to nine people) to 15 (five times three), and you will have used the time to create focus and equal sharing of speaking and listening time regardless of title and bias. Any and all of the ACE principles (Affirmation/Appreciation, Curiosity, and Empathy) can be easily integrated into how people converse, and you will have followed the S3 short-simple-small principle for interactions.

After the three rounds, having diverged people into small conversations, you can now debrief the group, less with "What do you think now?" than with "What did you hear from each other?" This approach of diverge-into-small-short-simple conversations and converge-back-to-everyone to aggregate the knowledge of the group taps the individual and independent perspectives of the group while surfacing novel and uniform ideas. It also mitigates the loudest voice in the room by splitting people into rotating and infectious conversations and asking them to pay attention to what they *hear*, not what they think. This final simple twist helps move them toward sensing and away from projection of their own bias. Further, you are mixing people into different combinations of give-receive dynamics so they can be heard, hone their own thinking via both repetition and added nuance as they both speak and listen.

Having done that with one interaction rule, you could start with another, "What do we need from each other to work most effectively together on this priority?" or "Who else needs to be involved?" and within a few minutes create clarity about what you all are doing, what is needed, and who needs to be involved via nearly 50 short and energizing interactions.

At any time during the work, you could engage people similarly to find out how they multiply interaction in their teams, when they themselves are and are not around, what they are noticing, learning, and how they and their team are adapting their capacity for individual participation and collective excellence. You can multiply yet again by rotating roles that people have within interaction patterns. Typically, our roles tend to be static, as do our spots around a table. Just as you can remove the table, you can move the roles. Although you would not want a software engineer to try being an air traffic controller for a day, having team members switch nontechnical roles within and across teams does wonders for people's receptivity to other points of view. If someone is typically a skeptic, ask that person to facilitate; it someone always facilitates, ask that person to observe the room's interaction dynamics. We rotated meeting and presentation roles frequently in the healthcare organization at Memorial, and people liked it so well they translated the practice to other teams they were on.

The following list provides some examples of how to multiply effectively and how to avoid some common traps. As you practice multiplying the numbers of spaces, participants, interactions, and interfaces, you will certainly discover your own iterations to these themes.

Principles of Multiplying

- DO introduce and practice interaction rules within conventional topics and approaches such as formal decision-making and meetings.
- DO use interaction rules when mixing groups.
- DO break up longer pieces of work with brief interactions to enhance focus or prevent lapsing back into less effective shared habits.
- DO encourage people to create, test, and share interactions that are ACE-based, S3, and applicable to their work.
- DO invite people to share how their rules are shifting PLV and inviting others to create PLV easier, faster, sooner.
- DO continue exploring for new rules that may enhance infection and contagion of patterns that support PLV.

- DO mix, mix, mix: combinations of people and teams, across boundaries and in multiple and unexpected combinations.
- When mixing groups, create many small, 1:1 interfaces and keep creating new combinations.
- DO NOT introduce too many new rules at once: try a couple for a while and see how they work.
- DO NOT block people's volition in using rules. Invite them to pick some and create some of their own.
- DO NOT confuse mottos and conditions with rules: "Growth Mindset" is a condition; asking "What did we learn here?" at the end of every discussion is a rule.
- DO NOT let rules come from only one person or only one group of people. Invite everyone to create, test, and share locally.

There is literally no end to how you can link interaction design, multipliers, and real work. Just as you can create mixed-gender pairings or diverse working groups, you can use these same techniques when you're putting different teams together to work on something important, designing interaction that intentionally multiplies the number of cross-team interfaces to multiply the transfer of perspective, technical knowledge, curiosity, empathy, and new patterns of thought, action, and interaction that are known to one team but new to another.

When I have seen multipliers used in this way, I am always reminded of the energy and enthusiasm that pours out of people who just minutes before were plodding like zombies through another markless day. In Uganda, I used this approach to get the teachers and staff talking about what they saw in the children. With the language barrier, the lack of familiarity between me and them, and the novelty of the topic, I would have had very little in response if I had interacted singly with the group, no matter how relevant my inquiries or sincere my curiosity. There were other forms of resistance I didn't recognize at the time as well, which is always true. For example, I didn't realize there was a significant difference between the teachers and the support staff—they typically didn't spend much time working with each other as much as they worked next to each other.

Nonetheless, when they all had a chance to rotate in and out of one-on-one conversations, I had trouble pulling them apart, which is always the case. One question I had asked them to speak and listen on was a leadership lesson they had learned as a child, which had stayed with them but which they had never shared with their colleagues. From the smiles, laughter, frowns, and nods I could see as I watched came multiple small but powerful stories that clearly had never surfaced in their work with the children. Midway through our reconverged debrief came another common statement, always unique to the group that observes it: "We have not ever done this. We should do this more often."

It is tempting to see this kind of work as cute but not practical. Both the behavioral research and the neuroscience suggest that such approaches are as essential as they are effective. What we all recognize in our own best team experiences is that P = Performance, L = Learning, and V = Vitality rise from the multiplying of the little things that make work *work*. The world of employee engagement has been rapidly changing during the last decade, and companies like Waggl and Glint now offer platforms for designing, surfacing, and applying social intelligence.

Our outstanding safety results at Memorial included some large issues that plague all of health care, but many more of them were tiny things only noticed in small observations and micro-interactions that our multiplying huddle was able to surface, address, and diffuse across our system far more rapidly than if we had made a long list and marched it through our more traditional monthly quality meeting. By thoughtfully using the multiplying effects of creating more interfaces within and across teams, as well as the principles of divergence-convergence, time-sharing in listening and speaking, and convening people into small conversations where they biologically *have to* connect with their conversation partners (and find it informative and enjoyable!), you can create both the diversity of experience and perspective and the experience of unity and coherence that make your growing epidemic solid and able to grow further.

Loop Backs to Loop Forward

Chapter 6 discussed the creation of reflection-action loops in interactions as an evolution of feedback and a key part of the arc from awareness to action. Such loops can also be used as multipliers to build forward from all kinds of interactions. In our ongoing example of 10 people in a room, one multiplying interaction might be to invite people to try similar approaches in other spaces where the 10 of you are not gathered. In essence, this exportable approach benefited the Growth Groups leads very well. They lead and facilitated a particular Growth Group of 12 or so members in pairs (diverged) and gathered (converged) as a group of Growth Group leads to debrief and shape their next approach. Demonstrating Surowiecki's four essential principles of collective intelligence, they had space and time to go to decentralized local environments, do their own observing and acting, and return to aggregate what they had learned, thereby allowing each of them a deeper experience from a unique environment and the ability to swap best ideas that could diffuse back to any and all of the groups. The larger Growth Groups' experiences constantly benefited from diverse and adaptive approaches and sifting of what worked and what didn't to diffuse lessons learned.

Creating a "feed forward" multiplier that prompts people to cluster their own group interactions into smaller conversations and time periods with designed time for listening and talking, diverging and converging, helps move participants from "enjoying the ride" when you are facilitating to creating that experience as leaders. A great forward multiplier is to establish that a group diverging out to try these techniques in other environments will use the four magic questions—*What happened? How do we know? What did we learn? Where next/how next?*—both within their "satellite" cluster and when you all reconverge from those separate spaces. As with all epidemic attempts, you do not need all nine other people in our hypothetical scenario to do this perfectly or completely. Simply setting up the multiplier and the loop creating public inquiry and attention to how their own multiplying efforts are going will create positive pressure by way of a steady stream of stories, triumphs, and challenges. Keep doing it, and people will influence one another.

Multiplier Practices

- DO
  - adjust pathogen as necessary
  - add spaces
  - invite more people
  - maintain conditions
  - increase the number of interactions per unit time and space
  - sift and reflect
  - diverge/converge

- DON'T
  - create complicated interaction container and melt people down
  - put an infectious particle out alone without conditional/social support
  - add more conditions, generally, at least not in terms of effort and recall

How Leaders Leverage Multipliers

The point of multiplying is to increase the prevalence, the total presence, of positive disease in your population, which you do by increasing the number of PLV interactions per unit time per unit of population in your system. Our two people in a locked room do not help that happen no matter how hard and often they cough or harangue. As is the case with designing micro-interactions, the leader's role is to model multipliers, both by example and by setting up patterns that can be observed, adapted, and diffused.

Because complex pathogens require repetition and social support to turn into actions and then into habits, multiplying actually happens in two axes. One axis of multiplying is "down and in," the repetition of engagement, reflection, and attempt as individuals move along their own uptake arc of new thoughts, actions, and interactions. These "internal multipliers" amplify the infection of a positive pathogen *within* people so that infection can express itself as the behavioral actions of positive disease. The second axis of multiplying is "up and out" as individuals move the pathogen back and forth between each other, honing the interaction patterns that accelerate and widen contagion.

Both these axes reinforce each other, as more infected people tend to act more contagiously and more contagion causes more infection. In addition to observing your own effect as an example of multiplying in your system, a significant aspect of your attention should go to helping people see, sift, and select the patterns that emerge. As always in complex environments, self-organization will create novel variations. These "mutations" can be helpful, boring, or harmful, and their unpredictable nature often inhibits leaders from letting interactions and multipliers run in their organizations.

As we established the Trust Cycle at Memorial, our neonatal intensive care unit stepped up and wanted to begin shifting their interaction patterns very early. They would not have been a space or cohort where I would have chosen to multiply early. We did not have a lot of momentum yet, and the Trust Cycle's viability in our system was fragile, even though its applicability was strong. Nonetheless, the NICU wanted to go, and they became a strong multiplier themselves in infecting other units who were initially more skeptical. On the other hand, I arrived one day for work and found a rock on my desk. On it were painted the words "*BS Trust.*" Mutation is an unpredictable thing!

Like designing micro-interaction, multiplying is an interactive alchemy, grounded, as the other epidemic actions are, on listening and observing. Complex adaptive systems are always sensing, sensing, sensing, and so will you and your colleagues as you release multipliers. This sensing and sifting is different from tabulating data (although you may wish to track your epidemic with data); you will have all the information you need if you have built short, simple, small feedback loops. Designing interaction requires an intense focus on the micro and its shift from a thousand daily inertias to unique but effective patterns of relating. Multiplying requires that we add focus to how we begin to link repetitions within a group and contagious extension from one. Multiplying also requires leaders to shift their own focal length back and forth from micro to macro and from the details of one environment to the similarities and differences among many.

If interaction design is about setting the prototypes for future patterns, multiplying is about linking those patterns and sifting through them for the inevitable better approach and the early disaster. The effect of multipliers is what allows pathogens to mutate and evade detection and treatment; the same effect allows us to create vaccines and cures for disease. Similarly, the feedback from the multiplying interactions will give you helpful information that may prompt you to shift your pathogen's antigens, your epidemic's supportive conditions, or the tenor and location of your interactions and containers. In a way, you will be setting up an interaction rule with your epidemic itself: "What do you, epidemic, need from me or us? What do I or we need from you?" Complexity will emerge into full dance as you multiply.

By continually sifting these emerging patterns and building multipliers that invite and compel others to do so, you will begin to see your epidemic take place at a larger scale, acutely infectious and contagious within small spaces and between people, but increasingly capable of attracting and connecting larger and larger numbers. As your epidemic multiplies, you will begin to see the micro-freedom and meta-stability that Keith McCandless and Fisher Qua write about in *Less Mystery, More Magic*. Like any other biological phenomenon, your job is to link your own local work with wider selection and sifting of environments.

We like to say, "Practice makes perfect." Technique-savvy practitioners say, "Perfect practice makes perfect execution." The growth-minded epidemic leader understands that practice with feedback loops creates both more stability and more opportunity. You will have a choice about whether you want to control this ambiguity by preventing it or embrace it as a path to PLV capacity beyond the surly bonds of a mechanistic organization. Choosing between epidemic and more formal approaches is not an either-or decision, but the willingness to embrace epidemic action as a worthy complement to our conventional mindset certainly is. While we think about it and wonder if it could really work, clouds of microbes in our guts and swarms of electrons in our computing clouds are already working this way and have been for a long time now.

Notes

1. Damon Centola, *How Behavior Spreads: The Science of Complex Contagions* (Princeton, NJ: Princeton University Press, 2018), 35–37.
2. Teresa M. Amabile and Steven J. Kramer, "The Power of Small Wins," *Harvard Business Review*, May 2011, `https://hbr.org/2011/05/the-power-of-small-wins`.
3. Jeffrey R. Young, "New Study Shows Where 'Growth Mindset' Training Works (and Where It Doesn't)," *EdSurge*, August 7, 2019, `https://www.edsurge.com/news/2019-08-07-new-study-shows-where-growth-mindset-training-works-and-where-it-doesn-t`.
4. Young Ji Kim et al., "What Makes a Strong Team? Using Collective Intelligence to Predict Team Performance in League of Legends," *CSCW 2017: Proceedings of the 2017 ACM Conference on Computer Supported Cooperative Work and Social Computing* (February 2017): 2317, `https://mitsloan.mit.edu/shared/ods/documents/?DocumentID=2710`.

5. Ishani Aggarwal et al., "The Impact of Cognitive Style Diversity on Implicit Learning in Teams," *Frontiers in Psychology* (February 7, 2019), https://doi.org/10.3389/fpsyg.2019.00112.
6. A. W. Woolley et al., "Evidence for a Collective Intelligence Factor in the Performance of Human Groups," *Science* 330, no. 6004 (October 29, 2010): 686–688, https://doi.org/10.1126/science.1193147.
7. Kim et al., "What Makes a Strong Team?
8. Alex "Sandy" Pentland, "The New Science of Building Great Teams," *Harvard Business Review*, April 2012, https://hbr.org/2012/04/the-new-science-of-building-great-teams.
9. "Collective Intelligence: Number of Women in Group Linked to Effectiveness in Solving Difficult Problems," *ScienceDaily*, Massachusetts Institute of Technology, accessed January 21, 2021, www.sciencedaily.com/releases/2010/09/100930143339.htm.
10. Andy Greenberg, "Mining Human Behavior at MIT," *Forbes*, August 12, 2010, https://www.forbes.com/forbes/2010/0830/e-gang-mit-sandy-pentland-darpa-sociometers-mining-reality.html?sh=732f505f7c7f.
11. Eric Garton and Michael Mankins, "The Pandemic Is Widening a Corporate Productivity Gap," *Harvard Business Review*, December 1, 2020, https://hbr.org/2020/12/the-pandemic-is-widening-a-corporate-productivity-gap.

9 Networks: The Ultimate Multiplier

About a year into our efforts at Memorial to diffuse the Trust Cycle as a positive pathogen, we were starting to see some pretty good results. Our lean efforts were leveraging it, and it was helping us improve performance within and between teams. Individuals and teams were learning how to learn faster from each other and from within. People were using simple rules to interact more effectively, and they were creating interactions that worked in their teams and discarding ones that were not fruitful. Import and export of those interaction designs between teams and units were bubbling as well. Where it was working, energy was rising. One day a nurse walked into my office with a compelling idea.

"I have a question for you," she said. I was happy to see that, unlike the first few people who visited my office in the earliest days of my tenure, she seemed quite at ease.

"Sure, I'd love to hear it."

"Well, do all the executives have coaches?" The expression on her face told me that she knew the answer.

"Is that the question?"

"No, that's the question before the question. I know the chief nursing officer does, because she told us, and she told us the COO has one."

"Interesting and true. Yes, they all have coaches. It's to help us maximize the kind of leadership we need." I could see her question coming, but she was patient. "What do *you* notice?"

"Well, we notice they're doing things differently. Asking more questions, giving people more room, asking us to create solutions and come up with ideas. So we asked. So FYI to you, although I'm sure you know—it's working."

"That is good to know. I notice it, too, in them and in the people I listen to around the organization, but it's always nice to hear."

"Well, here's my question. If coaching is helping them, why doesn't every leader have a coach?"

"I'm thinking you have an idea what I might say."

"I'm thinking you're going to tell me these are really important positions, and the resources for coaching go there so they can benefit everyone, because we don't have the money for every leader to have a coach."

"If I answered your question that way, what would you think?"

"It would make sense, but it wouldn't feel very good."

"Well, I'm not going to answer that way."

"You're not? What are you going to do?"

"I'm not sure yet. I think we should wrestle with your question."

"Okay." She nodded her head once, her eyebrows up a bit. "Fair enough."

"Do me a favor," I said. "Think it over yourself and talk to some of your people. If you were to get a coach for everyone, how would you do it?"

A few days later, Laura Quinn, my epidemic colleague, and I were talking in my office during one of our frequent conversations about how to accelerate transformation. We were reflecting on the pockets of resistance and uptake that both seemed to have their own momentum.

"I'm wondering how we can go faster without hurrying," I said. "It would be nice to go faster without going harder. Create a tailwind, not another box to check. A nurse dropped by the other day and asked a very compelling question—Why doesn't every leader have a coach?"

"What did you say to her?"

"Well, I didn't tell her what she thought I'd say, which is that we only have enough resources for certain people to get coaching. It's a great question, 'How do we scale coaching?' The exec team is chewing on it, and for that matter, so is the person who asked me."

"Why don't we put some team coaching in place?" Laura suggested. "We could link teams with coaches, spread the money out, and get people learning together and out in the open at the same time. Multiply the interaction rules in those containers."

I liked that idea and wanted to stretch it further. Our place was still siloed, and we needed more boundary crossing and diffusion. "Maybe we could link formal coaches with randomized groups, pull people across disciplines into learning-coaching groups. Mix things up; people who don't work together often or know one another very well, if at all. Create a normalized Trust Cycle experience relatable to their day-to-day efforts."

"I like that," she said. "You'd get coaching support, public exchange of learning in small groups, and create new connections where people don't typically connect. Who would you offer it to?"

"Every leader we have," I said. "Use the coaches, the group's own issues, and the Trust Cycle to get things rolling, and tell the coaches they have three sessions to get the clusters to self-sustainability. Maybe bring them back six or seven rotations later to help these new groups stay on keel. They don't have to teach the groups to be formal coaches, just to be stable crucibles where mixing of these interaction principles can gain traction and loop out to their work environments and back."

With that conversation, Trust Teams was born, a PLV accelerator that was the most highly valued thing we did in all our leadership development efforts. Every two weeks, every leader in the organization aggregated into groups that typically did *not* work together. Almost like Alcoholics Anonymous groups, the Trust Teams were without titles or hierarchy, just groups of six to eight people who led *something* and gathered with a certified coach. They had two hours to use the Trust Cycle pathogen and effective interaction rules to share insights, questions, difficulties, and possible approaches to PLV in and across their areas. They'd try the ideas out in their "native" work environment and return in two weeks to consider, in effect, the four magic questions: *"What happened? How do I know? What did I learn? What next?"* Plenty of sidebar chitchat in the spirit of "The New Science of Building Great Teams" flowed spontaneously during and around these get-togethers.[1]

At the time, I was primarily thinking of the benefits of mixing, horizontal cross-linking, and dense interaction to create new positive pressure and support around the shifts we were asking leaders and teams to make. Looking back, I realized we created a series of networks. We had created open-ended connections back to their work teams, but we could have been more imaginative and strategic with those outside connections. Had we been a bit more strategic and knowledgeable about networks at the time, we could have used the structural and social value of network design even more.

Biology, the operating system of all life on this planet, assembles itself via and into networks and networks of networks. Everywhere we look in the biological world, big and small, we find networks. Our bodies have neural networks, vascular networks, digestive networks, pulmonary networks, and renal networks. These networks comprise small branches converging into bigger ones and then diverging back again from big to small. These networks are, in turn, linked together in terms of their signaling so that we can go about our day raising our kids, meeting deadlines, creating new products, and foraging for food at the grocery store. Tree branches and roots are networks, and we now know that trees themselves are networked together underground via a co-network with fungi that allows them to create a kind of tree-to-tree nutrition exchange.[2] Elephants and whales have long distance communication networks that they use across vast spaces.[3] Apropos of anything that moves through biology, epidemics make their way through networks, and yours will, too.

Networks do not have to be biological, of course. Air travel routes, bus routes, supply chains of all kinds, computing technology, and communication platforms all comprise networks. Because of the social nature of our biology, we cell-network humans organize our activity into networks. The ubiquity of networks cannot be underemphasized as a dimension of epidemic leadership. As Nicholas Christakis and James Fowler point out early in their seminal work *Connected: The Surprising Power of Our Social Networks* that networks shape each of us, and we, in return, shape our own network.[4] Further, not only do our friends, or network contacts, connect us, our friends' friends' friends affect us. Think about that for a second (and read the book!). Further, networks have properties that cannot be explained by the actions of individual members.[5] By now we recognize this "more than the sum of its parts" property: networks demonstrate emergence.

"Network" has become a ubiquitous term, and "networking" is a requisite professional, political, and social activity these days. For the leader of epidemics, networks have unique utility and capacity. Collective intelligence is an emergent property of human networks, for example, and networks can be configured to incubate both wholehearted human improvement, volition, and meaning—all the things our brains thrive on—and high-powered PLV. Networks can accelerate your epidemic or, vexingly, grind it to a halt. Although networks themselves are neither good nor bad, their properties dictate that they don't spread or inhibit all things equally, a cautionary point for the leader who seeks to leverage them. As Damon Centola observes, "Social networks that accelerate the spread of an infectious disease can slow the diffusion of its cure."[6] Measles, for example, is really easy to catch, but the same networks that are susceptible to measles are resistant to changing their antivaccine views. Knowing how to tap networks and how to outflank their stunting effects on your epidemic combat will vastly deepen your understanding of how to diffuse epidemic effects.

Although every network is unique, networks have definable and patternable properties that create insights for leaders who create epidemics that will move because of and in spite of those networks. The research on networks the last two decades and especially more recently has surfaced startling and practical insights that help leaders understand diffusion and resistance in populations. Networks in our daily lives—the internet, local computer networks, social networks on Twitter, Instagram, Snapchat, and Facebook, transportation networks, distribution networks, transportation networks, and professional networks—have become phenomenal multipliers of both helpful and concerning phenomena. Finally, they are not optional. They are ubiquitous and omnipresent.

Network Implications for Epidemics

Networks are simply patterns made up of nodes and connections. The nodes may be computers, cells, humans, or molecules. The connections can be communication channels, blood vessels, chemical bonds, or electrical signals. Networks are defined by their structure, or *topology*; by the nature of their nodes and connections; by their content; and in human networks, by the interaction patterns in the connections between nodes. Again, they are also defined by emergence—the qualities that emanate from them that are not housed in any constituent part.

This book does not remotely articulate in total the deep and evolving knowledge on human networks and their impact on individual and network behavior, but a few basic concepts are essential for our exploration of how leaders can leverage networks to multiply infection and contagion and to mitigate the resistance against positive pathogens. The science and the math around networks is compelling and a worthy exploration for those who seek to understand more deeply how individuals and networks act and interact.

Networks Have Structure, Called Topology

All networks have structure, and that structure influences network properties. The childhood game Telephone, which really seems quaint and dated these days technologically, is a temporary network with a linear topology. Although children can sit in the *shape* of a circle or a triangle to play it, the *topological structure* is a straight line: information moves from one end to the other. Such a network cannot be exponential—the very point of the game is that signal, in the form of the first student's original message, distorts as the message passes through an increasing number of nodes.

Other networks are highly efficient at moving material or information and have come to dominate our mental model of shared work. The bronchial network of our lungs, for example, is unbelievably efficient at taking source material—ambient air filled with life-essential oxygen—and this network, powered muscularly by our diaphragm and the intercostal muscles between our ribs, effortlessly transfers air to the millions of tiny air-blood interface sacs we call alveoli. The lungs really function as a double network. On inhalation, they effectively distribute oxygen (and anything else mixed in with air) to the periphery of the lungs; on exhalation, they move air laden with $C0_2$, and any other gases in our blood stream (like alcohol) back out through the same network, moving that CO_2 from millions of alveoli out through the central exit point of the mouth and nose. The bronchial tree—all those branches from the main breathing tube known as the trachea all the way down to those millions of alveoli—has the same structure on inhalation and exhalation, but it moves very different content in one direction versus the other. In essence, it functions the way we draw organizational charts: one- or two-way flow of thought, action, and information.

Still other networks are more shapeless and chaotic looking, with abundant, occasional, or rare connections between tighter clusters, which may themselves be loosely or tightly connected. Infinite topologies are possible and present in the universe: spirals, blobs, blobs of blobs. The connections between nodes in a network are called ties, and these ties can be strong or weak. In human networks, strong ties are the ones we have with people with whom we are close—friends, family members, close co-workers. Weak ties connect us to people with whom we interact with less familiarity. Strong and weak can also refer to the frequency with which we bump into these people. Of course, any of us can be connected to people who don't know each other at all or to people we know who also know each other. Clusters or networks in which the ties are supported by cross ties between the members of other ties demonstrate high transitivity. Those clusters characterized by ties that don't redundantly connect are low transitivity. Think of transitivity as density in networks; put another way, in dense or highly transitive networks, everybody is connected to everybody.

There can be ties between these different clusters or neighborhoods as well. If there are many discrete ties between different clusters, the "bridge" between the cluster is wide; if there are only one or two ties between clusters, the bridge is narrow. The interplay between strong and weak ties and wide and narrow bridges has profound implications on the spread of both simple pathogens, like game scores or weather reports, and complex ones, like the patterns of thought, action, and interaction that leaders cultivate, grow, and ultimately stabilize.

Let's take a closer look at what happens from a network topology standpoint when a team implements some of the observed practices detailed in "The New Science of Building Great Teams." The two practices mentioned in Chapter 8 were primarily about how team members interact, but there are three others that define network structure. Those practices are that every team member connects directly with *everyone* in the group, that there are back-channel "before the meeting, after the meeting" conversation within the team, and that team members explore connections outside the team and bring back ideas or information.[7] Figures 9.1a and 9.1b delineate the network effect such activity has on a conventional hierarchical team. In effect, these practices convert the "org chart" team from a triangular distribution network, much like our

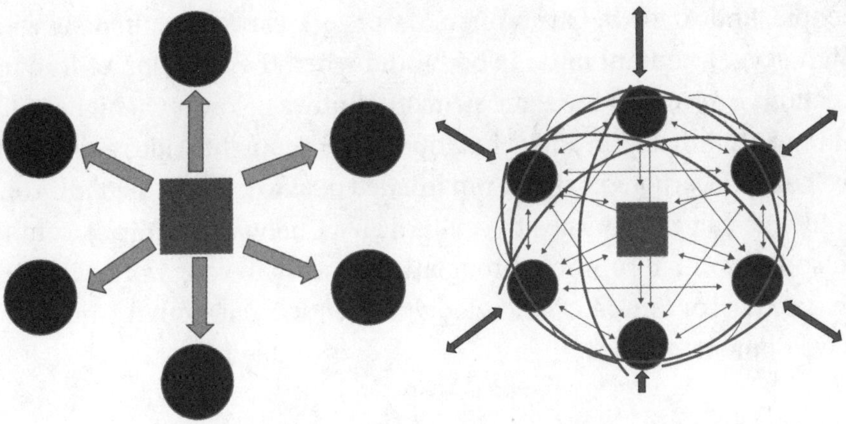

Figures 9.1a and 9.1b: Delineate the network effect such activity has on a conventional hierarchical team

bronchial tree, mentioned earlier, to a small network with abundant close ties and high transitivity (everyone is connected to everyone). Further, abundant weak ties (and potentially strong ones) are created outside the team. By applying these "structural practices," teams, and teams of teams, alter their network structure.

Network Content Counts

Two networks can have the same structure, the same array of nodes and connections, but do very different things. One network may be focused on getting out the vote, and the other may be interested in selling Girl Scout cookies. Mapping their ties, number of connections, topology, and transitivity would give you exactly the same image but their function would be entirely unrelated, unless of course we were to find that Girl Scout cookies made people vote more readily or that voting made people more likely to buy Girl Scout cookies.

Further, networks do not have to carry only one type of content. A network of AAU basketball teams presumably would traffic in a lot of basketball content, but it could also move thoughts and behaviors around public service, travel options, prioritizing nutrition for young people, and so forth. Our bronchial network carries inspired air with high oxygen content into the body, and when the direction of its connections is reversed, the same structure traffics in lower O_2, higher CO_2 air. In both inhalation and exhalation, other "content" rides along with oxygen and carbon dioxide, from inhaled dust to exhaled alcohol. Your epidemic can carry its positive pathogen as "new content" adjacent to the other content running through the network in your work, whether that other content is IT knowledge, revenue cycle activity, business development, or sales.

Networks Have Interaction Rules between Nodes via Connections

Beyond structure, connections, and content, networks have their own interaction rules. Again, the structure, connections, and content between any two surgical units or any two automobile manufacturing plants may be identical (in reality, any two networks are never exactly alike structurally unless you force that function, as they do in military squadrons, for example). One operating room may have interactions between individuals that are based on the ACE interaction principles, and the other might have a "do as you're told and don't ask questions" style. Those two networks would have the same structure, content, and connections, but perhaps very different function as a result of their interaction design within those structures and connections.

Nodes Count, Too!

In some kinds of networks, the nodes that are connected are relatively constant. In a network of sodium chloride crystals, for example, all the nodes are either sodium with a positive charge or chloride with a negative one. Humans are different, and their position in a network determines how many other humans they connect with, either as senders or receivers, but humans themselves are more or less effective at "nodeness." Recalling our identical structural networks with get-out-the-vote content or sell-Girl-Scout-cookie content, in either population will be people who are more or less effective at what they do as individuals and more or less contagious in how they relate to others in the network. To epidemic leaders, these contagious people have value in terms of *where* they are in networks, in terms of what *kind* of network they are in (linear vs. exponential, transitive vs. intransitive), but they are also more or less valuable simply because of their *ability* to create localized contagion.

At Memorial, as our "new rules" uptake of the Trust Cycle increased, we saw more and more people who were very capable of creating positive local effects. Like the Growth Groups founders, they emerged as hot nodes in our organizational array. They were not necessarily in our bronchial tree-like formal org chart network, but their emergence gave us the opportunity to think about how to leverage their skills in and across networks.

Help That Can Hurt : How Networks Influence Contagion

Research shows that happiness is a contagious property of networks. You are 15 percent more likely to be happy if one of your direct connections is happy, 10 percent more likely if one of your secondary connections is happy, and 6 percent more likely to be happy if a third-degree connection (who knows a person who knows you) is happy.[8] No wonder group stressors like the pandemic affect us all, despite the differences in our material circumstances! If emotions are so contagious within networks, why isn't it easy to spread *anything* across a team, a company, or a community simply by sprinkling the right pixie dust of thoughts or behaviors onto a few people and letting the network do the rest? Why is Damon Centola's observation that the very networks that allow for the spread of simple contagions/pathogens also prevent their cure?

Classically, we thought that close, tight, redundant networks were good for holding disease, while long ties were good for introducing it. The American sociologist Mark Granovetter theorized that "Whatever is to be diffused can reach a larger number of people, and traverse a greater social distance, when passed through weak ties rather than strong."[9] Intuitively, such diffusion makes sense; new ideas come from afar, they can reach populations of entirely new and unfamiliar nonimmune hosts, and things spread. It worked with smallpox disastrously for hundreds of years.

Unfortunately, weak ties actually *decrease* diffusion of complex behavior change.[10] It may seem counterintuitive to think that exposure to new and better approaches, or worse ones, are actually inhibited by contact with new ideas from new people, but the structural reason for that resistance is that weak ties inevitably connect to dense clusters of strong and redundant ties (think "closed circles") where the signal reverberates in a sort of echo chamber when it could be rippling out to new contacts rather than wasting time on ones that will simply recirculate within a small network.

In terms of behavioral resistance, infection with a new idea or way of thinking and its subsequent expression as action is a multidimensional neurophysiological shift in the brain, a kind of neural conversion—and it doesn't happen easily. The brain is wired to continue its habits and biases—after all, they have worked so far (or we think they have). New ways of thinking, acting, and interacting require more than just a passing thought or a casual exposure. Measles and COVID can spread via weak contacts throughout dense clusters, but not so for innovation, altruism, or collaboration. Infection and contagion of these complex pathogens doesn't happen in one fell swoop without multiple attempts, slides back to old tendencies, and renewed steps forward.

Exposure is important, but so is acceptance, insight, attempt, and social reinforcement. Changes in thought and behavior require conscious energy until they become habitual practice, and that effort must be supported intrinsically and extrinsically. The number of exposures counts, but so does the number of people who embody a phenomenon we hope will become contagious. To become receptive to change, we need to hear it often and from multiple people we find credible and influential.

Centola lists four factors that support why thought and behavior change require a number of sources, not just a number of exposures.[11] The first is an idea called *complementarity*: the concept that a behavior is more economically or practically valuable according to how many people practice it. Think about smart phones—if one person has one, you can't really use it to communicate, because no one is there to answer your texts or send you one; if everyone has one, it's a requisite item for communication.

The second factor is *credibility*. The more people are doing it, the more believable it is that it's actually beneficial or worth the hassle. The number of endorsements from credible people count. We are more likely to trust a cardiac surgeon on matters of heart surgery and an auto mechanic with our car, and if multiple doctors opine about medical issues or multiple auto mechanics recommend particular car maintenance, so much the better. Infection with COVID doesn't care who you heard it from or how many people you know who have it. If you're exposed, by anybody, you are at risk.

The third factor is *legitimacy*. The more people adopt a behavior the more you'd expect affirmation, validity, or at least less criticism. If more people have done something before you have, your receptivity to the idea goes up. Fashion works this way, which explains why we may think a style is really ugly, but when everyone else is wearing it, plenty of us do the same.

The final is *emotional* resonance. It's fun to be part of a crowd. Emile Durkheim studying the buzz that worshiping crowds create and feel, called this collective effervescence. Humans are attracted to shared emotional experiences. It's one reason we call people and say, "guess what just happened to me?!"

In experimenting with ways to leverage these properties, Centola validated the idea of a "wide bridge" between networks, where a bridge is a person who connects two different networks, and wide refers to the number of cross-network connections. Wide bridges involve many people crossing from one infected cluster to an uninfected one. Having just one emissary, no matter how contagiously credible that person is, cannot create the social influence to optimize shifts in behavior or to overcome local social resistance. It can happen, but the effort is heroic, not likely.

These structural wide bridges have to be supported by social relevance, the idea that the people/ties that are bridging the new behavior are like us, a term called *homophily*.[12] Of course, if you can cross those bridges often enough and with the right interaction design, you can create stronger ties as well as leverage the structural advantage of the wide bridge and actually create homophily as people realize they are, after all, quite similar. For all these reasons, WW (formerly Weight Watchers) works to help people lose weight—it creates a positive social network.

All these dimensions of networks are at play within and between networks. Further, networks can come entangled, stand alone, and coexist in layers. Our identical get-out-the-vote and sell-Girl-Scout-cookies can layer exactly on top of each other or exist somewhat out of phase, with certain members and relationships overlapping while others remain separate. Networks are also mutable and can be stable, unstable, or ephemeral. The people in your epidemic are part of an epidemic network, but they are also simultaneously members of many networks at work and in their personal lives. Some of those Girl Scout cookie sellers are involved in getting out the vote, and some are not. The structures and tendencies of these abutting networks will necessarily impact the epidemic you cultivate.

Leveraging Networks to Facilitate Contagion

Hoping that the networks in and around your epidemic will create beneficial effects will leave you at the mercy of all the dimensions of networks. You may end up lucky, as natural epidemics are, but recall also they have millions of chances and are usually simple pathogens. Since leadership epidemics spread complex pathogens and you don't have the time natural epidemics do to wait for innumerable variables to come together, your epidemic will benefit from a few simple principles that will allow your epidemic to grow and adapt. These same principles will give you room to experiment, observe, and sift the results of the principles against the behavior of the networks in your world as pathogen, interaction design, and multipliers interact within the larger incubator of networks where you are working.

Map, Model, and Move

As early as possible, even before your pathogen is on the move, take an inventory of your networks. Such an inventory can be done with sophisticated mapping software or simple observation around questions such as "Who are two people in this organization you really trust if they tell you something you're uncertain about?" or "Who do you go to for better ways to do things?" The answers will be necessarily incomplete and varied, but they will help you create a map of sorts. Subsequently create a network audit. Which networks are more likely to embrace and grow your positive pathogen early, which may be more cautious, and which are likely to harbor resistance? What do you know about the density and overlap of connections within and across networks? Are the bridges between networks narrow and confined to one or two people, or are there opportunities for wider bridging?

Such a network audit, crossed with the strategic and operating priorities that will influence where you start, can help you build a pathogen-seeding map. The map will change as your epidemic bubbles and creates its own momentum and resistance, but starting with a map and an intent to map, model, and move will allow you to think spatially about best places and ways to let your epidemic bubble on or intervene more actively.

To leverage established networks, ensure that there is wide exposure and immersion in your chosen conditions and interaction designs, and unleash the foundations of intrinsic motivation—mastery/improvement, volition/autonomy, and meaning/purpose—surface early adopters. As we did with our IT department and as we discussed in Chapter 8, facilitate as much frequent and iterative mixing of individuals; connections will be strengthened and new ones will be made. In effect you will be mimicking neuroplasticity and new synapse creation on a social scale.

Toward the conclusion of our three-day IT hackathon at Memorial, the one to which each IT associate invited an outside stakeholder, we all gathered outside the building, and Keith McCandless asked us to each to reach out and touch the shoulder of someone who helped us with an insight and whom we now trusted a bit more. What resulted was a powerful snapshot of a human network that did not look at all like the org chart of the formal relationships that had walked in the room. Redundancy and wide bridges abounded, and it was clear we had reconfigured our ability to tap new and newly shaped stakeholder relationships. As you launch and grow your epidemic, get clear about which networks are really in play in your epidemic world, for better and worse.

Get People off Narrow Bridges and onto New Islands

You will find plenty of people will resonate with your new pathogen, while others will wait and see and still others will more actively resist. Nothing says you can't create brand new networks of people who are resonating around the new pathogen, new interaction rules, and multipliers. These people are precious growth stock for your epidemic wherever they are and whatever they're doing.

The Growth Groups founders essentially hacked a bunch of email lists, culled them for early-in-hire people, and invited a mixed group of people necessarily curious and motivated, as well as connected to different networks inside the company. The pandemic later helped them mix up an even more diverse but motivated network by forcing them to go virtual and freeing them from physical location. Our Trust Teams were an accidental creation of new networks that essentially built wide bridges within our leadership group. Neither Laura nor I were thinking about networks and wide bridges at the time, but imagine the bridging and social support we could have helped design both among Trust Teams and among the teams and their home networks, aka teams and divisions. People will likely start autonetworking around their affinity for the pathogen, the conditions, and the interaction rules; nudging this phenomenon with some supportive design can create benefits for your PLV epidemic.

Make Homophily Happen

You will recall that the first element of our Trust Cycle, identified by our employees and springing from their personal experiences of their best team experience in difficult conditions, was the idea of common ground. We worked hard to equip people to identify and create common ground in a relational way. Many times we define ourselves by differences, which can occlude the beneficial social pressure required for complex change. If kidnappers and hostages can bond (albeit dysfunctionally), apparently different people can discover common ground. For the purposes of lower resistance and increasing trust, almost any positive interaction with a resonant experience will do. Asking people to tell the story of their most embarrassing moment, their best team experience, the best lesson on leadership they learned in high school can all connect people over the idea that we are really not that different. Remember, whenever we build the smallest bit of trust, we release oxytocin, that chemical that creates good will and the sense of bonding.

A great way to create this people-like-us perspective of familiarity is to intertwine wide bridge strategies with weak links. Move people who have become infected with your pathogen around to different areas, taking care to ensure that the I'm-just-one-of-you credibility will be authentic. Mix people from different areas and perspectives in small but multiple interfaces. For example, if you have two large groups of people you want to infect each other and create contagion within their teams, bring multiple people from each network together in cross-team small connections. Mix those connections so that you have a "knot" of people who trust each other and have the human mass to leverage their own groups. You don't lose any points for coaching both wide-bridge links and weak links on how networks respond positively and negatively to such structural interventions. When they bomb, it is obvious. When they hit the mark with the people they connect to, it's equally obvious.

These approaches can be effective flipping networks as well, but you will need more patience. The same principles apply, but so does the polarity of divergence-convergence. In a fascinating study, Centola took two polarized groups of Democrats and Republicans who were overwhelmingly misreading data on the subject of climate change and put them into social media interaction groups by overt political identity, subtle signs of politicization (an elephant or donkey on the screen), and anonymous identity. The data and discussion made no difference in the groups migrating toward shared and accurate data interpretation except in the anonymous groups, where 40 Republicans and Democrats spontaneously depolarized and correctly interpreted the data.[13] In other words, anonymity *enhanced* collective intelligence. The researchers were shocked at the fragility of the group's newfound insight, however. The minute the logos and trappings of party reappeared, the consensus shattered, even though it had emerged through egalitarian, participative dialogue.

It's tempting to want to isolate maladaptive networks and wall them off from your epidemic. Although a strategy for dealing with them is important, isolation can backfire. In the body, cancer is a maladaptive and dangerous network less because it exists and more because it has cut its signaling connections to the other networks and influences of the body. Operating rogue, densely connected to its own processes and disconnected from the body's healthy ones, these rogue networks multiply without yield, and death results.

For resistant groups, diverging into smaller conversations and creating interaction rules that "strip" participants of their roles and get them talking and listening as people with a common context is essential. As much as we like to think we make decisions based on data, we make them on emotions and belongingness. Create belongingness in small nontribal interactions, and you can begin to cross-pollinate resistant networks with more generative connections.

In Masese, it would have been foolhardy to try to get all the schools to embrace creativity and tree planting as a path to economic innovation and agroforestry. Nonetheless, as schools in the area have visited one by one, they've become curious about how HELP school did it and whether they might be able to also. The tree suppliers realize a wide bridge when they see it and are seeding the new schools without charge via the multiple human bridges from HELP school to the others. Trees are growing in one school (Figure 9.2) and are about to root and grow in many more.

Figure 9.2: Trees in HELP schoolyard

Killer App: The 3D Network

Given that wherever you are growing an epidemic to support PLV, your network is really an interwoven and overlapping conformation of many networks with different clusters, structures, content, and relating rules. Trying to make it finite and predictable in a rigid sort of way will render it unhelpful in both spreading complex pathogens and in teaching you how it can help or hinder such efforts. The ideal network, or network of networks, in your epidemic is diverse, dense, and diffuse, giving you lots of opportunities for design and observation. Diversity invites the kind of thought capital that will never exhaust itself; density gives you plenty of focus and momentum for your epidemic to have staying power, and a diffuse, sprawling territory will give you and your fellow epidemic makers rich opportunities for the novelty and credibility that weak ties bring. Your ability to tap, create, and mitigate networks to enhance the processes of infection and contagion will be key to the power of the epidemics you and your colleagues will be able to create. Wherever your network landscape starts, the networks themselves are mutable and flexible over time.

The work on networks is amazing, provocative, and continues to evolve. Networks are not new, but our understanding of their structure, behavior, and impact has exploded in the last few years. They make it easy for simple pathogens and hard for complex pathogens, and this is a challenge because patterns of thought-action-interaction are complex pathogens, and many harmful ideas are simple pathogens that move with the speed of rumors. For these reasons, leaders often abandon network approaches because it's easier to "hardwire" by fiat rather than the more emergent and self-organizing approaches of networks. Networks can certainly reinforce our human social tendency to deny opposing viewpoints and to refute reliable data, but they can also be used to create intense focus and wide adaptation in an organization. At varying times, your epidemic will require either or both, and will summon you to learn the path of the network weaver.

Notes

1. Alex "Sandy" Pentland, "The New Science of Building Great Teams," *Harvard Business Review*, April 2012, https://hbr.org/2012/04/the-new-science-of-building-great-teams.
2. Britt Holewinski, "Underground Networking: The Amazing Connections Beneath Your Feet," National Forest Foundation, May 28, 2019, https://www.nationalforests.org/blog/underground-mycorrhizal-network.
3. University of Vienna, "Mystery of Elephant Infrasounds Revealed," *ScienceDaily*, August 3, 2012, https://www.sciencedaily.com/releases/2012/08/120803103421.htm; David Brand, "Secrets of Whales' Long-distance Songs Are Being Unveiled by U.S. Navy's Undersea Microphones—But Sound Pollution Threatens," *Cornell Chronicle*, February 19, 2005, https://news.cornell.edu/stories/2005/02/secrets-whales-long-distance-songs-are-unveiled.
4. Nicholas A. Christakis and James H. Fowler, *Connected: The Surprising Power of Our Social Networks* (New York: Little, Brown Spark, 2009), 17–21.
5. Ibid.
6. Damon Centola, *How Behavior Spreads: The Science of Complex Contagions* (Princeton, NJ: Princeton University Press, 2018), 7.
7. Pentland, "The New Science of Building Great Teams."
8. Christakis and Fowler, *Connected*, 51.
9. Mark S. Granovetter, "The Strength of Weak Ties," *The American Journal of Sociology* 78, no. 6 (May 1973): 1366, http://links.jstor.org/sici?sici=0002-9602%28197305%2978%3A6%3C1360%3ATSOWT%3E2.0.CO%3B2-E.
10. Centola, *How Behavior Spreads*, 40–41.
11. Ibid., 38–39.
12. Ibid., 143.
13. "Can Social Media Networks Reduce Political Polarization on Climate Change?" Annenberg School for Communication, University of Pennsylvania, September 3, 2018, https://www.asc.upenn.edu/node/5705.

10 Technology and Epidemics

Technology is a useful servant but a dangerous master.
—Christian Louise Lange

Today's leaders create PLV value in environments that are increasingly not just supported by technology but integrated with it. Automation, smart devices linked into the Internet of Things (IoT), artificial intelligence (AI), cloud computing, online marketing and social media, and virtual hosting are all normal in nearly every sector. Your epidemic won't just have to move through and around technology; it will have to create a distinctly human experience in an era when we are already in chimeric human-technology settings. We don't just have bionic parts; we have bionic workplaces. The question for leaders of epidemics is how to leverage technology to support the organizing principles of your epidemic when that same technology has profound promise and peril for the uptake and spread of the thought, action, and interaction underpinning PLV.

The very real promise of technology in speed, reach, convenience, and bandwidth has been steadily yielding ground to the realization that, particularly in the mining of usage data, the farming of our attention, and the erosion of nonvirtual experience, technology casts an ominous shadow on individual and societal health and well-being. Increasingly we are seeing neural effects and substantive changes in how humans relate in a world in which much of our communication and relating is through a screen.

With regard to social media, the fluid and anonymous nature of the platforms have ambiguous effects. In *Bowling Alone,* Robert Putnam argues that this fluidity and anonymity, the ability to get in and out quickly, creates an environment where "trust, commitment, and reciprocity will not develop."[1] On the other hand, we've seen the benefits of interactions that are fluid and "de-identified" in the Chapters 7–9 on interaction design and in Centola's study on how anonymous discussion chat rooms helped polarized political players come to a common and correct interpretation of data on a controversial and polarizing subject.

Our social media and internet communication also allow previously anonymous voices, individuals, or groups to gain and create social capital very quickly. Although the barriers for entry are low and Instagram, Facebook, LinkedIn, and YouTube are packed with endless (and time sucking!) content, individual influencers clearly gather significant followings and subsequent social significance. Who knew that being an influencer could be a profession? These platforms can support the rapid aggregation of status and legitimation—and revenue. According to *Forbes* magazine, Evan Fong logged over 1.5 billion views on YouTube and hauled in $11.5 million from 2018 to 2019 for his videos of *Grand Theft Auto* and *Minecraft*. He was number 10 on their list of top-10 YouTube earners. The highest earner was eight-year-old Ryan Kaji at $26 million, who got his start on his own channel at age three opening gifts.[2]

Clearly the internet can generate views and revenue, but it offers more than that. The QAnon conspiracy flourished because of online accrual of social legitimacy around a false idea, but so did the Kindness Pandemic. Founded March 14, 2020, by Dr. Catherine Barrett, the group grew to 500,000 people in two weeks and is dedicated to supporting victims of COVID-19. Both the website and the Facebook page encouraged people to set up their own #thekindnessepidemic groups and guidelines for doing so. Major sponsors jumped on board, and so did major media, according to the organization's website.[3] The Founder's message? "Acts of kindness are infectious," Barrett says.[4] Clearly technology can help the epidemic leader.

Of course, there is the shadow side of all this technology for those who seek to scale PLV integrally and not extractively. Our social media and communication technology afford unparalleled speed and broadcasting ability, with speed of transmission clearly an advantage for spread—of some things. That same speed and the ability to aggregate large numbers of users and watchers, coupled with technology's impact on attention space would seem to favor simple pathogens, the kinds of things that can quickly be "liked" and passed on before reflection and diligence come into play. The number of conspiracy theories and outright misinformation, both well intended and more maliciously seeded, illustrate the power of these platforms in aggregation and dissemination. They speed the spread of content by making it easy to "like and pass" before the slower reflective part of our brains can reflect and sift.

The internet can certainly speed, aggregate, and distribute contagions, but which ones? The technology itself is ethically agnostic a priori, a thorny problem that many technology companies are struggling with internally and in terms of customer and political perception. No bit of inside-out storytelling relates this ambiguity better than *The Social Dilemma*, the excellent documentary by the Center for Humane Technology, featuring the insights and vulnerable observations of several tech founders, engineers, and executives.[5]

Trying to lead epidemically in this age without using technology thoughtfully seems as naive as creating a new energy grid using candles and matches. Instead, understanding the risks and advantages of technology to your epidemic and to its human co-creators is essential. Designing your epidemic for maximal technological benefit and minimal technological risk, like all things epidemic, will be an interactive and learning experience. The jury is still out on neural, relational, cultural, and sociological effects of our social media technology. The ethics of data mining and the conversion of customers, always the holy grail of business, to commoditized (if customized) data substrate are topics of rising concern, and clear risks are emerging.

Technology Risks to Positive Epidemics

Disinformation

We used to talk about transparency, with the implicit implication that there was a known and universally supported body of knowledge. Any one of us may not *know* all that knowledge, but it was out there, like a cube or a vault, and transparency was key. Transparency is still important, particularly in the micro-interactions of your epidemic, where deception is certain to undermine infection and contagion at the interpersonal level. Because positive epidemics root, rise, and grow on the integrity of micro-interactions, aggregated into collective intelligence, they should afford a hedge against internal disinformation if intelligently designed. On the other hand, misinformation certainly does flourish and diffuse rapidly in the online space and whenever it affirms the emotional support of a person's or group's identity. Recall the University of Pennsylvania study on Democrats and Republicans and how quickly the anonymous chat participants devolved away from the truth once it became clear they were on opposing sides of a political divide. The COVID pandemic has been rife with misinformation, with at least one study linking susceptibility to disinformation to decreased likelihood of trusting the vaccine or following health guidelines.[6] Disinformation has real world impact. On Twitter and Facebook, just 12 accounts were responsible for 65 percent of misinformation on those platforms,[7] and social media users were more likely to believe disinformation regarding COVID.[8] Savvy agenda-mongers of all stripes realize the real power of disinformation: if you repeat it enough times from enough sources, it will be perceived and defended as truth. As a simple pathogen, misinformation carried by online technology is a formidable epidemic indeed.

Diminished Attention

Anyone who has tried to have a conversation with a spouse, child, or co-worker while they are on their phones has noticed what research is demonstrating: screens grab our attention, and our attention is fragmented. Studies show that learning and memory suffer as a result.[9] In a study of over 2,500 adolescents, high use of digital media was associated with a higher prevalence of ADHD symptoms over the next 24 months.[10] As we think about the necessary engagement of the mindful brain in shaping neuroplasticity and subsequent changes in thought and action patterns necessary for behavior change at the individual and group level, threats to attention become threats to the vigor of positive epidemics.

Degraded Relatedness

The virtual environment delivers unbelievable advantages for collaborating over distance, simulation of technical skills, interviewing, telehealth, development coaching, and more. Nonetheless, we risk connecting our brains increasingly to our screens and electronic networks rather than to our bodies. Particularly when we understand how technology companies intentionally used the neural-reward feedback loops to capture our attention,[11] we realize our devices lead us further from the live environment of our native biology. I have seen wonderful hi-def video of elk and giraffes. I have been lucky to see both of them live and in the wild as well. Whatever the high-density video and high-resolution sound in the virtual experience, it is a sensory sliver of seeing those things alive and real and present. As sophisticated as our screen lives are becoming, and as much as we tout the virtual experience, the virtual world cannot deliver the touch of a hand, a pat on the shoulder, or the immediacy of eye contact. We think of the virtual experience as rich, but compared to actual live experience, it is quite sparse. The impoverished screen environment has been associated with diminishing creativity, focus, and reflection,[12] all key ingredients in the relational phenomenon of a positive epidemic. One wonders if such a less-textured reality might favor simple pathogens and discourage complex ones via virtual transfer as a result.

Anti-Emergence

As the use of technology grew as a method of communication, numerous observers were concerned our experience might fragment into echo chambers where we encountered only views we agreed with or topics with which we were familiar. Cass Sunstein (2001), in the book *Republic.com*, specifically addresses this concern, arguing that "the most striking power provided by emerging technologies [is] the *growing power of consumers to filter what they see* [emphasis in the original].[13] Although the concern of echo chambers remains and is certainly supported by the clustering of social influence around unfounded ideas online, research shows that people do encounter a diversity of ideas online and views and perspectives different from their own.[14]

More recently, we've begun to see the seductive power that social media technology has on our attention, a fact that conspires with the production of "user-driven" content to narrow our total experience of living, whatever its diversity or richness online. Such capturing of our attention is not accidental.[15] "The short-term dopamine-driven feedback loops that we have created are destroying how society works," Chamath Palihapitiya, a former Facebook executive, says on an online interview. "It literally is a point now where I think we have created tools that are ripping apart the social fabric of how society works. That is truly where we are. I would encourage all of you, as the future leaders of the world to really internalize how important this is. If you feed the beast, that beast will destroy you."[16]

The questions about ethics, narrowed online exposure, and addiction aside, we are at risk for living a designed life rather than an unfolding one. In the world of biology and humanity, we might describe life unfolding as Explore, Experience, Examine. We get up every day, and we step out into the unknown. Our curiosity and commitments guide us, and events find us. To the extent we choose, we reflect, learn, reminisce, adapt. It may feel familiar, but we do not know what is ahead of us. The universe is unfolding, and we move in it. Online, we might describe our experience as Search, Sort, Select. The two might seem similar, one real and one virtual, but our online searching determines what comes to us to sort and select—a universe built *around* us.

Given the essential element of emergence in our lives and in epidemics, such a designed "user experience" has ominous undertones. We need things to "pop up" inexplicably from the sum of our actions. When the online world is built around our whims and activities, we are essentially minimizing the chance of emergence, serendipity, and surprise, all elements critical to the growth of humans and epidemics alike, uncomfortable as those realities might sometimes be. Whether this kind of narrowing is consumer driven or data mining may not really matter.

Anti-emergence, the designed minimization of the surprises, quirks, and unpredictabilities of our social activity, will certainly confine epidemic action. Epidemic leaders focus on cultivating biodiversity of participants and possibilities, not prospectively narrowing them to the perceptual biases of the current state.

Leveraging Technology to Support Epidemic Action

Inviting, Broadcasting, and Convening

When Growth Groups got going at Microsoft, the initial groups were able to get together live—once. After that, the early epidemic was chased into the virtual space by the COVID pandemic. As one might expect from a cohort of digital natives, the groups moved seamlessly to virtual get-togethers and virtual keynotes. They actually found that they could convene *more* people. Initially, they planned to invite only people from the proximate geographic location of the founders. Virtual convening allowed them to invite anyone and group them by time zone.

What the virtual conferencing platforms lack in physical presence they compensate for with reach. In effect, they provide a compelling container where many of the activities of epidemic action are quite effective. As leaders and network clusters create stories of epidemic action and their impact on local PLV, technology affords an easy medium for broadcasting stories in a compelling and attracting way. Growth Groups was able to broadcast internally, but they also posted on LinkedIn.[17] These platforms offer powerful advantages for widening the circle of invitation and story-based feedback loops within and from the virtual communities themselves. Given the open-system nature of epidemic action itself, these platforms have the added advantage of supporting nearly unlimited scaling of both interaction and containers.

Numerous businesses and start-ups have leveraged these approaches to break previous barriers and invite new participants into entrepreneurial activities. All-Turtles, Atomic VC, and Backstage Capital are all examples of entrepreneurial platforms that are leveraging technology to invite new entrepreneurs and investors beyond the usual candidates.

Mixing Things Up

It would seem that technology, with all its speed and distance, would favor simple pathogens that don't require effort, practice, and social support to spread. On the other hand, it is relatively easy to define the homophily that people gravitate to as they think about change. With a little effort, it is almost easier online to create mixture across differences while creating a sense of "we are like each other." Simple interaction design such as having people join with cameras and microphones off and then mixing them together in varying combinations with varying interaction-rule questions via chat functions can create a sense of "I belong here."

You can turn the cameras on at any time, of course, and splitting people into small one-on-one conversations, well-designed, is an easy way to create the multiple small interfaces that support affirmation, curiosity, and empathy of the ACE principles. On most platforms, you can begin clumping people together so you create both diversity of experience and a deepening sense of common ground across otherwise prohibitive distances. I have been impressed, both as a facilitator and an attending participant, at how multiple mixing of small conversations works online. It has the added benefit of keeping people very focused on one another as well. Refusing to talk with your conversation partner online is as obvious as it is in person!

Designing Interaction

In some ways, the distributed nature of technology platforms forces us to be better at designing interaction. I have been in large gatherings of several dozen people where we have split into small conversations and reconvened into large ones in multiple combinations and rounds. Nothing can match the rise in energy or Durkheim's collective effervescence of those live big-tent events, but it's also easy for people to get distracted in those large venues. Taking the time to design interaction is essential to leverage the advantages of the technology and overcome the disadvantages. Diverging into small conversations and reconvening into larger ones takes on a different dimension. More time has to be spent in smaller interfaces, and the general audience portions have to stay sharp, brief, and short. Using the chat function to synthesize feedback and trends is helpful, as is designing divergence *away* from the screen and back again through longer encounters. Ironically, you can use the technology to educate people about the wear-and-tear of being yoked up to a screen and encourage people to reflect on technology itself as a barrier to live human experiences.[18]

Mapping, Modeling, and Learning

One of the most compelling ways to leverage technology is to map networks and track how internal interventions and external conditions affect the structure and interactions within the network. Behavioral Analytics Retail lists 19 technologies that can track human movement and even interaction.[19] Various companies such as Waggl and Glint create crowdsourcing value. Primarily their technology is grounded in the 2.0 evolution of the employee satisfaction survey, but the point is that crowdsourcing capability is already available to help assay collective perspective and intelligence. A product called Avalon, by Twiin, actually tracks sentiment analytics.[20] Their focus is on patients and in healthcare, but being able to track participant sentiment as feedback loops about interaction effects and as predictors of shifts in patterns of thought, action, and interaction would vastly add to an epidemic's knowledge about itself in real time. Mapping your epidemic via network mapping software, available from numerous companies, provides an effective way to visualize your epidemic's underlying network architecture.

The link between human epidemics and our continually and rapidly evolving technology capabilities is inextricable. We will certainly see further technology in the future that can help us map and model epidemic action, and leaders will continue to lead teams that are essentially human-technology platforms, as automation and AI continue to grow as fields. Self-organization will not go away, and the need for leaders who can facilitate it and integrate it into more formal human processes and technology applications would seem to be a requisite need in a future in which complexity is poised to increase, not decrease. We won't stop needing to create epidemics—we will most certainly need to create ones that are epidemics of integrated human-technology form and function.

Notes

1. Robert Putnam, *Bowling Alone: The Collapse and Revival of American Community* (New York: Touchstone by Simon & Schuster, 2001), as quoted by Damon Centola, *How Behavior Spreads: The Science of Complex Contagions* (Princeton, NJ: Princeton University Press, 2018), 142.
2. Madeline Berg, "The Highest-Paid YouTube Stars of 2019: The Kids Are Killing It," *Forbes*, December 18, 2019, https://www.forbes.com/sites/maddieberg/2019/12/18/the-highest-paid-youtube-stars-of-2019-the-kids-are-killing-it/?sh=4472c5df38cd.
3. "About #TheKindnessPandemic," The Kindness Pandemic, accessed February 11, 2021, https://www.thekindnesspandemic.org/#/.
4. Christina Maxouris, "They Joined a Movement Focused on Kindness. Some Say It's Helped Them Get Through the Pandemic," *CNN*, February 22, 2021, https://www.cnn.com/2021/02/22/us/kindness-pandemic-facebook-groups-trnd/index.html.
5. *The Social Dilemma*, directed by Jeff Orlowski (2020, Netflix), https://www.netflix.com/title/81254224.
6. Jon Roozenbeek et al., "Susceptibility to Misinformation About COVID-19 Around the World," *Royal Society Open Science*, October 14, 2020, https://doi.org/10.1098/rsos.201199.
7. Audrey McNamara, "A Dozen Anti-Vaccine Accounts Are Responsible for 65% of Disinformation Shared Online, New Report Finds," CBS News, March 25, 2021, https://www.cbsnews.com/news/vaccine-disinformation-social-media-center-for-countering-digital-hate-report/.
8. Matthew A. Baum et al., "The State of the Nation: A 50-State COVID-19 Survey Report #14: Misinformation and Vaccine Acceptance," The COVID-19 Consortium for Understanding the Public's Policy Preferences Across States, September 23, 2020: 5–6, https://www.kateto.net/covid19/COVID19%20CONSORTIUM%20REPORT%2014%20MISINFO%20SEP%202020.pdf.

9. Jessica S. Mendoza et al., "The Effect of Cellphones on Attention and Learning: The Influences of Time, Distraction, and Nomophobia," *Computers in Human Behavior* 86 (September 2018), https://doi.org/10.1016/j.chb.2018.04.027.
10. Chaelin K. Ra, MPH et al., "Association of Digital Media Use with Subsequent Symptoms of Attention-Deficit/Hyperactivity Disorder Among Adolescents," *JAMA* 320, no. 3 (2018): 255, https://doi.org/10.1001/jama.2018.8931.
11. Nir Eyal, *Hooked: How to Build Habit-Forming Products* (New York: Portfolio/Penguin, 2014).
12. Debra Bradley Ruder, "Screen Time and the Brain: Digital Devices Can Interfere with Everything from Sleep to Creativity," Harvard Medical School, June 19, 2019, https://hms.harvard.edu/news/screen-time-brain.
13. Cass R. Sunstein, *Republic.com* (Princeton, NJ: Princeton University Press, 2001), 8.
14. Julius Matthew Riles, Andrew Pilny, and David Tewksbury, "Media Fragmentation in the Context of Bounded Social Networks: How Far Can It Go?" *New Media & Society* 20, no. 7 (March 2017): 1, http://dx.doi.org/10.1177/1461444817696242.
15. Chamath Palihapitiiya, interview by Stanford Graduate School of Business, *View from the Top*, November 13, 2017, https://www.youtube.com/watch?v=PMotykw0SIk&t=1298s.
16. D. B. Dillard-Wright, "Technology Designed for Addiction: What Are the Dangers of Digital Feedback Loops?" *Psychology Today*, January 4, 2018, https://www.psychologytoday.com/us/blog/boundless/201801/technology-designed-addiction.
17. Jay Li, "How University Hires Built a Startup within Microsoft (Part 1)," LinkedIn, March 22, 2021, www.linkedin.com/pulse/how-university-hires-built-startup-within-microsoft-part-jay-li/.
18. Jeremy N. Bailenson, "Nonverbal Overload: A Theoretical Argument for the Causes of Zoom Fatigue," *Technology, Mind, and Behavior* 2, no. 1 (February 23, 2021), https://doi.org/10.1037/tmb0000030.
19. Ronny Max, "19 Technologies of People Tracking," *Behavior Analytics Retail*, January 27, 2021, https://behavioranalyticsretail.com/technologies-tracking-people/.
20. Doug Arbittier, personal conversation with author, October 20, 2020.

11 Toward Positive Pestilence

If you want to win, build a platform.
—Reid Hoffman, paraphrased

'Tis the times' plague, when madmen lead the blind.
—William Shakespeare, King Lear

This book has been about how leaders can think about the design and dynamics of epidemics to facilitate patterns of thought, action, and interaction to multiply performance, learning, and vitality at every level. As we end our conversation on creating positive epidemics, I want to spend some time on the kind of epidemics we need from the kind of leaders we need. Both leadership and epidemics can be transactionally effective but ethically unmoored, and as a doctor, father, and grandfather, my emphasis is on exponential growth of health and sustainability for land and people. Anyone can learn the skills in this book, either at the level of basic proficiency or shamanic elegance, but we need more than just the ability to create practical scaling of PLV if we are to shape a healthier world for ourselves and future generations.

The science and practice of epidemics as a leadership model may seem a bit niche, apropos of and applicable to the two-pizza rule, the loose rules of start-ups and innovation, or cost effective and undisruptive ways to engage otherwise less-productive employees in a world of relentless productivity and talent attrition. It is tempting to think of epidemics and their dynamics as quaint adjuncts to the hard edges of business and leadership rather than to embrace them in a deeper context—as a widely applicable leadership platform for stability, adaptation, and emergent wisdom in complex landscapes.

By 2012, the Trust Cycle Epidemic at Memorial Health System, like most epidemics, flourished for a time and then disbursed. During its active phase, a $650 million organization created a $100 million turnaround within 24 months during a recession, without having any structured layoffs. Quality improved threefold, and the community of Colorado Springs tackled a 30-year untouchable topic of what to do with its health system, ultimately leasing it to University of Colorado Health.

Perhaps most poignantly, a janitor pulled me aside in the hall one day toward the end of my time there. The political forces of bureaucracy had closed in and the city was controlling decisions in the organization to "protect its asset" (an ironic posture indeed, considering that political behavior had put the organization at risk, and its people had grown its tangible and human value against those headwinds, but that is another tale altogether). It was clear my time was done. The man asked me how I was doing.

"Fine," I lied.

"You're not going to make it through this, are you?" It was phrased as a question, but he wasn't asking one.

"No, I'm not. But you will."

"You should know," he started, "that I have never spoken with any other CEO. What you brought here will not leave with you. It comes from all of us now. Keep that with you."

The Growth Groups Epidemic at Microsoft multiplies on, having surpassed 440 early-in-career participants by its fifth cohort (Table 11.1). The group has created wide bridges with the early-in-career demographic, senior leadership, and the more formal HR-anchored early-in-career (EIC) efforts within the gigantic tech company. In short, Growth Groups is on the verge of integrating into the DNA of Microsoft as a

Table 11.1: Growth Groups by Cohort, Microsoft; used with permission

Date	Cohort	# Members	# Leadership Team
Oct 2019–Jan 2020	1	77	5
Feb 2020–May 2020	2	461	19
June 2020–Sept 2020	3	1152	31
Oct 2020–Dec 2020	4	996	40
Feb 2021–May 2021	5	756	43

permanent mutation and an outgrowth and contributor to its growth mindset corporate ethos.

In Masese, Uganda, as of the Spring of 2021, the once-barren HELP school burgeons with young gardeners and future farmers, readying itself to export tree planting as education to waiting local schools. Pastor Frederick has infected his pastoral colleagues with creativity-as-pathogen through local bible colleges and pastoral training centers in Uganda (3), Kenya (2), and Mozambique (2).

Epidemics are more impressive for their universal approach to adaptive capacity than for their unconventional rules or their start-up visage. They do organize by unconventional rules, but only by our mechanistic definition of convention. They're not new rules; they're old ones. They are the same rules that govern the aggregation of online groups, Instagram influencers, and political polarization; the same rules that foment disease, unleash cancer, and fill the oceans with immense schools. We tend to think of epidemics as ephemeral and labile. Like the influenza that we know is coming every year, we see them as temporary and fleeting, perhaps not as the sterner stuff we need to learn and lead in a world of very stubborn and snarled challenges.

Epidemics, though they may flare suddenly, are not the opposite of stable and sustaining. The rapid and dramatic onset may look that way to us, but even the brief ones are sustainable and stable in their fidelity to the rules of biology, that operating system that sits on the planet's hardware of atmosphere, oceanics, and geology, as we all do. Many epidemics become permanent. Once they create an interface between pathogen and host, the two actually integrate, with or without an initial period of disease. Human papilloma virus (HPV), HIV, and tuberculosis are examples of pathogens that create a stable presence in our bodies and our populations, and they all enjoy long periods of latency before they cause disease.

We even know that viruses carry human genes as we carry virus-borne genes that are beneficial and necessary for human life,[1] unveiling the mixing of code between life forms that ebbs and flows like tides across our bodily borders. It turns out that we are more fields of matter and consciousness, open systems through which elements move and flow, than impenetrable objects. In this slow and infinite dance of life across our immune system's defensive boundaries, epidemics are not so much events as they are vectors that can carry us to new steady states. When they are successful enough, pathogens go from epidemic to *endemic*, permanently with us. We need new steady states right now and a new leadership platform to create those states from. We need to stabilize our societal DNA with new adaptive pathogens, or genetic upgrades of our current ones.

We live in difficult times. We can point to the valuations of stock markets, the amazing number of innovations in medicine, energy, communication, and technology as evidence of positive progress. We would not be wrong, but we can also point to the flashpoints of human conflict, population compression, marginalization of human communities, the degradation of planetary biodiversity, and the erosion of civic discourse. At the same time, we recognize that beneath the logistics of the very real issues we have to address, we fragment to polarization rather than unite with diversity. Whether the issue is our rancor over public health approaches to the COVID pandemic, our response to our history and present of racism, or our division over assertions about election integrity, our public discourse has become a froth of increasingly vehement assertion of our points of view and denigration of opposing ones. We can and should debate the substance and origins of this phenomenon, because the twin pathogens of avoidance and polarization are dividing our world when we can no longer afford the primitive luxury of tribalism.

The age of epidemics has arrived. It is no longer a tabletop exercise or a nerdy Bill Gates TED Talk. While we argued about masks and mandates, politics and procedure, public health and private rights, more people died in the United States than did combatants in World War I, World War II, and the Vietnam War combined.[2] The opioid epidemic, launched to support the insatiable and addictive hunger to dampen pain and abetted by profiteers who knew better, killed over 80,000 people in the year before mid-2020, a record high over the already-increasing total in 2019. Americans used to die from street heroin; now we die from opioids manufactured for commerce. The obesity epidemic rolled on as well and emerged as a significant synergistic factor in COVID mortality and morbidity.[3] According to the CDC, 34 US states have obesity rates higher than 35 percent in adults. Thirty-four states and the District of Columbia have an obesity rate of at least 35 percent for non-Hispanic Black adults; 15 states have a rate of 35 percent or higher among Hispanic adults; 6 states have an obesity of 35 percent or higher among non-Hispanic White adults.[4]

There are more epidemics, of course. Anti-Asian hate crimes, the disproportionate killing of African American men at the hands of police, mass shootings, and the rise of white supremacy. My overwhelming Saturday night in the ER has become the twenty-first-century steady state. Steven Hawking's century of complexity is here.

To adapt in this century will require us to scale particular capacities. We will need to multiply a shift in our fundamental mental and behavioral pathogens in a sea of vehement opinion with very few safe harbors of exploratory dialogue. We already have an abundant array of ideas, people, and possibility; scaling them and diffusing them widely across sectors and populations is the urgent challenge. On a planet heading toward 9 billion people, isolated heroic action by leaders will fail simply because of the insufficient social firepower of those good efforts. Industrial, mechanistic approaches that commoditize followers will fail because of the inability to invite the necessary authorship and participation. We've tried both these models in the nineteenth and twentieth centuries. They made for wonderfully inspiring personal stories and impressive gains in mass manufacturing, but they left us exhausted and divided.

We will need to permeate uncountable companies and institutions with the pathogens that create health and sustainability on an increasingly small planet. Argue and divide as we may, biology makes the rules, and physics and chemistry have determined this world as the only place where we can survive, and the only place we all call home.

Foundational Shifts from Leaders

At the level of specificity, the number of capacities needed for stability and adaptation within teams, companies, school boards, governments, and communities is unlimited. Education must focus on education, business on business, and governance on governance; revenue-cycle departments will pay attention to different things than IT and marketing. At the level of what works everywhere and allows seamless overlap between different technical proficiencies and different sectors, the following three capacities will enable epidemic action within groups to create internal worth while inviting interfaces across groups to scale PLV globally. To go beyond transactional application of biological approaches to leadership, leaders will need to embody and propagate them in droves.

Collective Intelligence

If one of the miracles of self-organization is emergence, one of the emergent miracles of social human behavior is collective intelligence.

Not only is it real, but we know how to design it and replicate it.[5] Within our population we have a wide array of curiosity, insight, altruism, creativity, perseverance, and adaptability. The application of the science of collective intelligence taps the individual intelligence of group members but does not require uniform individual intelligence. The relational practices of teams define the team's intelligence and capability. Nonetheless, we continue to underutilize and under practice team intelligence. Our reliance on technical expertise and social hierarchy emerge as significant barriers to the unlimited benefits of collective intelligence practiced everywhere. (Wouldn't all of us appreciate and benefit from intelligent political bodies?)

The irony is that epidemics, mass swarms of witless particles streaming within and among us, manage the paradox of individual freedom and participation and collective intelligence and function elegantly. They demonstrate emergent "intelligence" with their relentless adaptability in a nonhierarchical interaction architecture. Collective intelligence is not subversion of individual value but amplification of it.

If the distorted perceptions of collective intelligence are coercive power, bureaucracy, communism and totalitarianism, designing collective intelligence is none of those things. In well-led epidemics, freedom, participation, and volition are integral to the value and stability of the whole. Biological pathogens create all these qualities without knowing all the theory behind them and so can people with the right leadership, support, and invitation. In well-designed social epidemics, inclusion begets diversity of participation and widely distributed equity of authorship and ownership. No one person is more important, and no one person is marginalized.

We seem to be wired for this kind of opportunity. Humanity has thrived ancestrally by virtue of collaborative intelligence (consider taking on a mammoth by yourself a few thousand years back), and scientists are now beginning to discover evidence of direct brain-to-brain communication. As the authors note, "This study opens the door to extraordinary new means of human collaboration while, at the same time, blurring fundamental notions about individual identity and autonomy in disconcerting ways."[6] These findings are hard to even imagine, but they emphasize the nature of our biology. We are designed as nodes in a network, a network capable of altruism, kindness, compassion, creativity, and innovation as well as selfishness, cruelty, violence, regression, and rigidity. Biology helps us understand that relatedness is not bondage; epidemics thrive on freedom of movement and collective emergence. Biology invites an evolved regeneration of human community.

Linking Homophily and Diversity

For decades, sociologists have noticed how humans gravitate toward and are more comfortable around similar humans. As the old saying goes, "Birds of a feather flock together." We know now that this idea of "homophily" is necessary in supporting behavior change in networks and in electing in which networks and groups we choose to gather. Unfortunately, homophily also has the disadvantage of sharpening the idea of "other," the people we don't understand, listen to, or migrate toward. In settings of power asymmetry, scarcity, or fear, *other* can quickly become "wrong and enemy," whereas *homophily* can mutate into "we are right, because we are us."

Are we doomed by homophily to aggregate in fragmented and apparently homogenous crowds online, howling at those who look different than we do or act or think differently? Will online networks split us into infinite warring tribes under the flags of group sanctity until we upcycle violence as our final collective act? What do we do with this thing, homophily, that glues us together so?

Wonderfully, no matter how different we humans are, we always share two immutable things. We are human, and we live in the same place. We have families, ancestors, and descendants. We want to live fulfilling lives, enjoy our neighbors, and celebrate our children. Homophily won't go away, and it becomes a huge asset if we can find ways to link differences under its umbrella. Epidemic action creates affinity among people, one by one, two by two, as people start with what they share in common and build up and out from that mutually created reality. We cannot replace homophily with diversity so much as build homophily underneath our diversity. In our bodies, a completely "homophilous" cell line, a group of cells exactly alike with no variation, de-linked from the signaling of the body and other cells, is called cancer. In biology, diversity is strength. In biology, lack of diversity is death.

More Biophilia

In nature, that thing we are part of but forget, every biological process cycles into another one, and every bit of biological material circulates out of one life and into another. This circular, waste-becomes-substrate and product-becomes-capital approach happens within our bodies as our spleens recycle red blood cells and we remodel the calcium structures of our bones, and it also happens between organisms, populations, and species. Animals expel carbon dioxide and take in oxygen; plants take in carbon dioxide and expel oxygen. The more we understand biology, the more we appreciate that it is the ultimate economy. Constantly stable, constantly exchanging, constantly abundant, wonderfully resilient to siege and surge. We would do well to emulate it for what it is—*the* operating system, not an optional political topic.

Epidemic Leadership as a Platform

Can we run our businesses, institutions, and communities with greater health and capacity with these principles? Is leading epidemically a gimmick or a platform, an option or a way? Can we replace the triple-stranded pathogens of acquisition-convenience-gratification and resentment-blame-marginalization that so plague our world with connection-contribution-gratitude and respect-understanding-inclusion? You get to decide. Epidemics have much to teach us about the uptake and diffusion or new mindsets into stable and widely held patterns. Biology demonstrates that performance, learning, and vitality will not just sustain but will multiply within epidemic frameworks and will degrade without them. To many, that difference is what we observe; to others, such frameworks are projections of pretension rather than insight for the future. If enough of us create the right kind of epidemics, the social momentum of our teams and companies, our societies and world, will make the truth known. Arguing will not generate the solutions we need; epidemics can.

The questions of how we lead and organize today are essential, and the possibilities of learning from epidemics are compelling to all who would seek to create a more effective, more sustainable, healthier world. I hope this book helps you unleash that epidemic. Whoever you are, whatever you do, wherever you start, however small or large your personal influence is, we need epidemic leaders. Now. Everywhere.

Notes

1. David Quammen, "How Viruses Shape Our World," *National Geographic*, February 2021, 47–48.
2. Jason Murdock, "How Many Americans Died in World Wars, Vietnam, 9/11 After Joe Biden's COVID Death Claim," *Newsweek*, April 8, 2021, `https://www.newsweek.com/joe-biden-covid-death-comparison-world-wars-vietnam-9-11-1575650`.
3. Barry M. Popkin et al., "Individuals with Obesity and COVID-19: A Global Perspective on the Epidemiology and Biological Relationships," *Obesity Reviews* 21, no. 11 (November 2020), `https://doi.org/10.1111/obr.13128`.
4. "New CDC Data Finds Adult Obesity Is Increasing: Obesity Worsens Outcomes from COVID-19," CDC Newsroom Releases, Centers for Disease Control and Prevention, September 17, 2020, `https://www.cdc.gov/media/releases/2020/s0917-adult-obesity-increasing.html`.

5. David Engel et al., "Reading the Mind in the Eyes or Reading Between the Lines? Theory of Mind Predicts Collective Intelligence Equally Well Online and Face-to-Face," *PLOS One* (December 16, 2014), `https://doi.org/10.1371/journal.pone.0115212`; Alex "Sandy" Pentland, "The New Science of Building Great Teams," *Harvard Business Review*, April 2012, `https://hbr.org/2012/04/the-new-science-of-building-great-teams`.
6. Robert Martone, "Scientists Demonstrate Direct Brain-to-Brain Communication in Humans: Work on an 'Internet of Brains' Takes Another Step," *Scientific American,* October 29, 2019, `https://www.scientificamerican.com/article/scientists-demonstrate-direct-brain-to-brain-communication-in-humans/`.

Acknowledgments

A lifetime of roaming clinical, corporate, and wild landscapes has graced me with a host of essential and invaluable mentors and muses. I want to thank foremost my partner in epidemic thinking, Laura Quinn, PhD, for her limitless curiosity and insight about what moves entire human systems, small and large and regardless of topic. Her combination of observational skills, integrated thinking, and willingness to converse over rambling scrawl on whiteboards made this book possible. I also want to thank Jim Kouzes, author of *The Leadership Challenge,* for stepping out of a crowd when I was presenting and giving me the positive nudge to write this book. Similarly, I want to thank Lisa Shannon of Big Sky Bold for helping me create a viable proposal out of what had been just an idea.

This book and my thinking would not be complete without the hundreds of people who have been willing to try things a different way with and around me. I especially thank the teachers, staff, and students at HELP primary school in Masese, Uganda, particularly Frederick Ojiambo and Ronny Sitanga in Uganda, and Jean Kaye Wilson, the founder and force of nature behind the school's origins, here in the United States. My profound gratitude to the Microsoft Growth Groups founders Michael Bervell, Jay Li, Aly Mirza, and Dan LaBruna, as well as early pioneers Revi Cheng and Rahul Surti. I left my interviews with them convinced the world is in good hands. Many thanks also to Juliana

Tioanda and Kareem Choudhry at Xbox Division at Microsoft for their executive insight on Growth Groups. I also want to thank Erika Yuag at Microsoft, who spent ample time talking with me about Mavericks, another emergent thought-action-interaction pattern within Microsoft.

I want to thank the good people at Wiley who helped me start and finish this, my first book. Particular thanks to Jeanenne Ray, Sally Clark, and my developmental editor, Adaobi Obi Tulton, who always seemed to be working at whatever hour I emailed her with questions.

I want to thank my family and particularly my wife, Ankie, for encouraging me to write, and for my four sons, who have made real and vital the relentless work to create a positive future. I thank master horseman and good friend Brandon Carpenter for all he has taught me about the confluence of biology, leadership, and development in the space of a round corral. I likewise thank my unusual black horse, Side Socks, who for 20 years has taught me the powerful wisdom of connecting without words on rough terrain.

I want to thank the patients, colleagues, and clinical mentors who shaped my thinking in places where people lived and died. Most of all, I thank my parents, who brought me out onto the ground in all kinds of weather from the time I was young and encouraged me to think about better ways to live and lead.

About the Author

Larry McEvoy is an emergency physician, healthcare CEO, and entrepreneur whose interests at the intersection of business, biology, and health have forged his thinking about the need to innovate leadership exponentially for the challenges of the twenty-first century. His work focuses on regenerating organizations, companies, and communities to exponential health and vigor—where performance, learning, and vitality rise in parallel and are abundant, infectious, sustained, and sustaining.

From 2008 to 2012, Larry served as the CEO of Memorial Health System in Colorado Springs, Colorado, facilitating a strategic and operational turnaround, the emergence of a culture of collaboration and commitment, and Memorial's transformation from an at-risk and unfunded municipal hospital to the threshold of its merger with the University of Colorado Health system. Prior to that he was a senior executive and emergency physician at the Billings Clinic in Billings, Montana, from 1995 to 2008. He completed his training in emergency medicine at Hennepin County Medical Center in Minneapolis,

Minnesota, in 1995. After earning a BA in English Writing from Carroll College (MT) in 1987, Larry graduated from Stanford University Medical School in 1992.

A storyteller and gifted facilitator, he is adept at convening groups to craft their own self-determined clarity and direction amid uncertainty or ambiguity. His career has comprised the renewal of multiple environments of distrust, stress, and dispirited dynamics. As a lifelong horseman, outdoorsman, and biologist at heart, he can be found—or difficult to find—as he stewards rugged country of Cove Canyon Grasslands to abundance in south central Montana.

Index